Basketball
Shooting

Basketball
Shooting

Dave Hopla

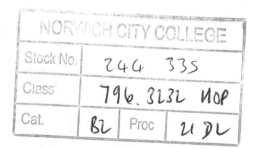

Human Kinetics

Library of Congress Cataloging-in-Publication Data

Hopla, Dave.
  Basketball shooting / Dave Hopla.
    p. cm.
  ISBN 978-0-7360-8737-7 (soft cover) -- ISBN 0-7360-8737-0 (soft cover)
  1. Basketball--Offense. 2. Basketball--Training. I. Title.
  GV889.H66 2012
  796.3232--dc23

                                   2012008016

ISBN-10: 0-7360-8737-0 (print)
ISBN-13: 978-0-7360-8737-7 (print)

The web addresses cited in this text were current as of April 2012, unless otherwise noted.

Acquisitions Editor: Justin Klug; **Contributing Editor:** Tanner Grover; **Developmental Editor:** Laura Floch; **Assistant Editor:** Elizabeth Evans; **Copyeditor:** Annette Pierce; **Graphic Designer:** Bob Reuther; **Graphic Artist:** Tara Welsch; **Cover Designer:** Keith Blomberg; **DVD Face Designer:** Susan Rothermel Allen; **Photographer (cover):** © Human Kinetics; **Photographer (interior):** Neil Bernstein; **Photo Asset Manager:** Laura Fitch; **Visual Production Assistant:** Joyce Brumfield; **Photo Production Manager:** Jason Allen; **Art Manager:** Kelly Hendren; **Associate Art Manager:** Alan L. Wilborn; **Illustrations:** © Human Kinetics; **Printer:** United Graphics

We thank Lake Land College in Mattoon, IL, for assistance in providing the location for the photo shoot for this book.

Human Kinetics books are available at special discounts for bulk purchase. Special editions or book excerpts can also be created to specification. For details, contact the Special Sales Manager at Human Kinetics.

The contents of this DVD are licensed for private home use and traditional, face-to-face classroom instruction only. For public performance licensing, please contact a sales representative at **www.HumanKinetics.com/SalesRepresentatives**.

Printed in the United States of America   10 9 8 7 6 5 4 3 2 1

The paper in this book is certified under a sustainable forestry program.

Human Kinetics
Website: www.HumanKinetics.com

United States: Human Kinetics
P.O. Box 5076
Champaign, IL 61825-5076
800-747-4457
e-mail: humank@hkusa.com

Canada: Human Kinetics
475 Devonshire Road Unit 100
Windsor, ON N8Y 2L5
800-465-7301 (in Canada only)
e-mail: info@hkcanada.com

Europe: Human Kinetics
107 Bradford Road
Stanningley
Leeds LS28 6AT, United Kingdom
+44 (0) 113 255 5665
e-mail: hk@hkeurope.com

Australia: Human Kinetics
57A Price Avenue
Lower Mitcham, South Australia 5062
08 8372 0999
e-mail: info@hkaustralia.com

New Zealand: Human Kinetics
P.O. Box 80
Torrens Park, South Australia 5062
0800 222 062
e-mail: info@hknewzealand.com

                                                              E4986

To all of my loved ones. Especially Mom (wish you were here to read it), my brother, Skip, my Aunt Jean, Aunt Joey, and Aunt Wezzy. Special thanks to my immediate family: my beautiful wife, Carole, and our beautiful daughter, McKenna.

Contents

DVD Contents

LONG-RANGE JUMP SHOTS

Three-Point Shot: Straight On

Coaching Point—Be a "Lifter"

Three-Point Shot: Off the Dribble

Three-Point Shot: On the Move

Game Situations: Shuffle Step

Coaching Point—Using Fakes When Shooting From Long Ranges

BANK SHOTS

Bank Shot Technique

Coaching Point—Determining When to Use the Bank Shot

Bank Shot Form Shooting Drill

Pull-Up Bank Shot Drill

CREATING YOUR OWN SHOT

Going by the Defender

Shot Fakes

Coaching Point—Reading the Defender

Jab Step

Coaching Point—Shot Faking and Jabbing Effectively

Step Back

SHOOTING AND SCORING OFF SCREENS

Shooting and Scoring Off Screens Technique

Coaching Point—Footwork Off the Screen

Around-the-World Spinouts Drill

Spinouts To and From the Baseline Drill

Left-to-Right V-Cut Drill

Baseline Shooting Drill

RUNNING TIME .... 50 MINUTES

The DVD included with this book will enhance your knowledge of basketball shooting. This DVD demonstrates the techniques and drills discussed in the book. The techniques and drills that appear on the DVD are marked with a symbol in the margin:

Acknowledgments

Without the Good Lord in my life, none of this would have been possible. Thank you to my wife, Carole for your love, support, and understanding. Thank you to my daughter, McKenna, for making me the happiest man on the earth with your inner and outer beauty, sweet smile, and wonderful sense of humor. Thank you to my mom who would have never believed I wrote a book. I miss you dearly. Not a day goes by without you in my thoughts and prayers.

Also, I would like to thank the administrators at every camp, school, and college who have let me speak about or teach the art of shooting. Thanks to Hank Slider, Herb Magee, and George Lehmann for all your inspiration. Tanner Grover, you are the best!

chapter 1

Shooting Philosophy

Over the past 40 years, being involved with basketball on every level imaginable, I've been fortunate to have had the opportunity to coach some of the greatest athletes to ever play the game and learn from some of the greatest coaches in the sport. Many of these basketball aficionados have shared with me their philosophies about how the game should be played and taught. For example, some coaches prefer zone defense, and others like man-to-man. Some preach a run-and-gun style, while others believe that championships are won in the half-court. However, when it comes to shooting a basketball, I have never heard of such discrepancies. Shooting is a universal skill, and the object is the same: put the ball in the basket. To ensure that players can shoot the ball well, coaches at all levels generally teach a uniform set of fundamental skills.

After listening to and working with those numerous coaches and players, I was able to become a better shooter, teacher, and coach. In terms of learning and gaining perspective on the art of shooting, I've absorbed lessons and ideas from players ranging from 10-year-old kids to 10-year NBA veterans. I've always kept an open ear and an open mind when it comes to shooting, and it's enabled me to take some of the ideas and philosophies from coaches and players at all levels and develop my own shooting philosophy.

If you purchased this book, you have an interest in becoming a better shooter or coach, or maybe you are a parent of someone who has an interest in the game. I have learned so much over the years that it became time for me to put it all together, right here, in this book, and it's all for you. By the time you're finished reading this, you should feel confident and more than capable of becoming or teaching someone how to become a great shooter. You never stop learning, coaching, teaching, or improving. And my philosophy extends from that final point.

Have the Desire to Improve

You can't just say that you want to shoot better. You must actually have the will, desire, drive, discipline, and patience to do this. Shooters are made, not born. Every great shooter has a great work ethic. Evolving into a great shooter requires you to spend more time shooting than the average player does. Shooting is a craft that takes countless hours to hone. However, simply putting in time is not the sole variable to becoming truly great. You must be willing to make changes and adjustments where necessary. Perfect practice makes perfect.

As a fan of basketball, haven't you observed someone shooting and said to yourself, "Wow, they have the perfect shot"? J.J. Redick, former

Naismith College Player of the Year for Duke and current three-point specialist for the Orlando Magic, comes to my mind as someone who has textbook form, or the perfect shot. Well, although J.J. is certainly an elite shooter at the NBA level, he is by no means perfect. In the 2009-2010 NBA season, J.J. shot 87 for 219 from behind the three-point arc. That's a 40 three-point percentage. That means he missed more than half of the threes he attempted. Last time I checked, perfect means, well, perfect, which would imply that someone never misses. By those standards, I would argue that J.J. has a lot of work to do.

I'm not trying to sound cynical. Far from it. But when it comes to shooting, I take an idealistic approach. I believe that perfection is something that should be perceived as attainable. As a shooter, I have the will, desire, drive, discipline, and patience to develop my shot in order to achieve perfection. That's the train of thought that I hope to pass along to you as you read this book. You see, nobody has the perfect shot, and until you can make every shot, there is room for improvement.

A lot of players think there is nothing wrong with their shots, yet they shoot poor percentages. Players who continually do the same thing and expect a different result are only fooling themselves. To me, that's the definition of insanity. First off, don't fight change; embrace it, especially if your percentage is low. And if you do, in no time you will improve. A common excuse that some kids will pull out of their back pocket when first making adjustments or changes to their shots is "It just doesn't feel right." That is completely understandable given the fact that they have shot incorrectly for so long. I'll often tell these players to compare their shot to a new pair of shoes. New kicks may not feel right at first, but once you break them in, they become comfortable. The same thing goes for your shot.

Unfortunately, though, too many players give up on adjusting their shots because they don't allow enough time for them to start to feel right. They might initially miss some shots and say that their new technique doesn't work and end up going back to their old ways. Do not settle for mediocrity. There is no excuse for shooting a low percentage, especially in your practice routines where you are likely unguarded.

Chart Your Shots

If you are committed to becoming a better shooter, you must chart your shots to help you see yourself getting better. If you go to the gym and shoot for a couple of hours, you won't know the facts and figures, such as how many shots you took or how many shots you made, unless you chart them. Charting your shots is easy. Keep a notebook and a pen in your gym bag, and when you hit the hardwood, record the number of shots made from a particular spot and how many attempts it took you to make those shots. For example, say I want to work on my corner three-point shot, and I want to make 25 from each corner. I shoot my shots, and then in my notebook I record "threes: RC (right corner), 25 for 30; threes: LC, 25 for 35."

Once you get into the habit of charting your shots, you will be able to see the improvement. It will be right in front of you in black and white. Once you see yourself improving, you will gain confidence. Confidence leads to success and success leads to confidence. It is an ongoing cycle. Also, being able to see improvement will encourage you to continue practicing. See chapter 10 for more detailed information on charting your shots.

Set Goals

By setting goals, you show that you are serious about improving. In the corner threes example, it would be apparent to me that I need to improve on that shot, especially from the left corner. Remember, I'm always striving for perfection. For me, 25 makes out of 35 attempts just isn't good enough. When I started out years ago, I set a goal of having to make five in a row from the three-point line before moving to the next spot. Now I make 25 in a row from the college line and 10 in a row from the NBA line. My new goal is to see page upon page of "25 for 25" charted in my shooting notebook.

Numbers have a way of motivating people. Whether it is how much money you make, what you want to weigh, or how many shots in a row you make, having a goal to work toward will help keep your motivation high so you can achieve a sense of accomplishment when you reach your goals. It all goes back to the cycle of success leading to confidence and vice versa.

Take Baby Steps Toward Improvement

If you can't make an unguarded shot close to the basket and without anyone defending you, how are you going to be able to make a three on the move with a defender draped all over you? When improving your shot, you need to take baby steps. Babies crawl before they walk and walk before they run; the same goes for your shooting practice. If you watch where most young players start shooting from when they run into the gym, you'll see that they head straight for the three-point line. Not only are they straining to shoot the ball, but they are also doing so with incorrect form and using every muscle in their body to force the ball up. In doing this, they are developing bad habits at a young age that only become more difficult to break as they get older.

To learn to shoot correctly, young players not only should start close to the basket but should also begin shooting at a lower basket and with a smaller ball. It is unfair to think that a young child can shoot correctly from the three-point line or even the free-throw line with correct shooting form and technique. For example, take a look at the sport of baseball, where kids begin playing tee ball and progress to underhand pitches from a coach or parent, and then on to Little League. We don't take our youngsters out to Yankee Stadium and expect them to pitch from the pitcher's mound. Use modifications when practicing with young players to help them learn to shoot the ball comfortably using correct shooting form and mechanics at an early age. This allows them to develop correct muscle memory and be more consistent with their shot as they mature.

Don't Rush the Development of Your Shot

If you're like most people, you want instant results. Unfortunately it takes years and years to become a truly great shooter, along with hundreds of thousands or even millions (yes, millions) of shots, all shot correctly in order to become a great shooter. Developing your shot can be a daunting task, and most people are impatient and don't want to put the time in. I swear, this is why the lottery is so successful: people don't want to work for their money; they want it to be handed to them.

With basketball, or anything for that matter, it all comes down to desire and how good or great you want to become. If you want to become a successful shooter, you can't rush the process of improvement and you cannot become frustrated when you miss a shot. Remember that everyone misses. Michael Jordan missed more than 12,000 shots in his career. Now this is a guy known for taking big shots with the game on the line. Talk about confidence! And Jordan missed many a game winner, but the beautiful thing is that no one seems to recall those games. We remember "The Shot" to beat Cleveland in the 1989 playoffs or the championship-clinching jumper in game 6 against Utah that capped off Jordan's career in Chicago in the most memorable fashion. Confidence is key. Realize that it is inevitable that you will miss, but how you react to that miss is what matters. Learn to use that miss as information, as important data. Did you miss short, long, left, right, or a combination of these? If you learn to use information about your misses in a positive way, you can determine why you miss. All of this is vital information for becoming a better shooter.

Visualize Successful Shots

Before you actually shoot the ball, you should learn to picture yourself shooting the perfect shot, which you never miss, visualizing the shot swishing and hitting nothing but the bottom of the net. Swish the shot. Don't just visualize yourself making it; swish it. Mediocre shooters try to make shots, but great shooters want to swish shots. It requires more focus and concentration, and you'll eventually discover that when shots rattle in, you won't feel satisfied. Visualize yourself swishing every shot. Picture yourself being on balance, feet shoulder-width apart, your shooting arm fully extended with the elbow locked out and above the eyebrow, your head still and eyes fixed on the target. Before you can be successful on the court, you must visualize yourself being successful on the court. When I played basketball in high school, college, and overseas, I always played the game beforehand in my head. I wanted to be ready for everything, and I wanted to have experienced it beforehand. Great players have great minds. See yourself being successful and you will be successful. See the ball going in and it will go in.

Strive for Consistency

When shooting, the ultimate goal is to be consistent in your shot, not hot and cold or streaky. To do this, you must develop good habits and eliminate poor habits so that you can achieve correct muscle memory. You will develop consistency by adopting a set practice routine. Every time you step on the practice court, you should begin by shooting a common series of shots close to the basket. This warm-up prepares you both physically and mentally and provides consistency in your shooting routine. Warm-up routines are important because they allow you to focus on your habits and the corrections you might need to work on, such as a flailing elbow or hand placement on the ball. Once you're warmed up, you're ready to take your shots. As described previously, charting your shots will help provide you with concrete information about the shots you're taking and the shots you're making so that you can work toward achieving consistency and better understand where improvement or adjustments are needed.

Also note that in order to be consistent on all areas of the court, you may need to spend more time in one spot than you might in others. Often, players tend to just practice where they are the most successful. We get it; you're a fantastic three-point shooter from the top of the key. How are you on the right and left wings or along the baseline? Work on shots that you have trouble making consistently. Pretty soon, your weaknesses will become your strengths. Also, mix it up. Spend time practicing and charting all types of shots, such as layups, midrange shots, three-pointers and free shots. Work on shots off the catch and also off the bounce as well, dribbling right to left and left to right. You can piece together endless combinations and routines. Put in the time, and you can develop consistency in a variety of shots.

Keep It Fun

It's important to remember that basketball is a game and games are meant to be fun, not boring. Some players might find themselves bored when working on their shot. Keep shooting fun by challenging yourself each and every practice. There are so many things that you need to work on and improve on that you should never become bored in doing so. Every time that you step on the floor, play games against yourself. For example, see how many shots in a row you can make from certain spots on the floor or how many shots you can make out of a set number or even how many shots it takes to reach a certain number of successful shots. You can also challenge yourself further by adding a time element and seeing how long it takes for you to make a certain number of shots. The next time you work out, try to beat your previous scores. By changing the number of reps or the amount of time, you change up your drills, keeping them new, refreshing, and fun.

Maintain a Positive Attitude

I can't stress enough that you should approach your workouts with a positive attitude. Sounds simple enough, right? Unfortunately, many players who put in the practice time often become frustrated when they fail to see immediate results. This all goes back to having the desire to improve. If you bring that desire, you bring with it a positive attitude. Every day that I step into the gym whether to shoot, lecture, or work someone out, I am excited about the opportunity that presents itself. Is today the day that I make all of my shots? Is today the day that I make more shots than I have on any other day? Is today the day that the player I am working out has a better day than he or she ever thought possible? If you bring a positive attitude to the gym, you will accomplish positive things. Understand that you and only you can control your attitude. So go ahead and make shots, not excuses.

I want to take a moment to review the key elements of my shooting philosophy:

- *Have the desire to improve.* Great shooters believe that there is always room for improvement, and they have the desire and work ethic to perfect their craft.
- *Chart your shots.* This allows you to actually see your improvement and gain confidence in your shot. Confidence leads to success and success leads to confidence.
- *Set goals.* Setting goals such as a certain number of shots to make in a row will keep you motivated, and achieving those goals will provide a sense of accomplishment.
- *Take baby steps toward improvement.* Begin shooting close to the basket and work your way out. Remember, babies crawl before they walk and walk before they run; the same goes for your shooting practice.
- *Don't rush the development of your shot.* You can't rush the process of improvement and you cannot become frustrated when you miss a shot. Instead, learn to use misses as data to help better determine what aspect you need to work on.
- *Visualize successful shots.* Picture yourself shooting the perfect shot, which you never miss, visualizing the shot swishing through the bottom of the net.
- *Strive for consistency.* Consistency is developed by having a set practice routine that includes a warm-up, charting your shots, and practicing a variety of shots from all areas of the court.
- *Keep it fun and maintain a positive attitude.* Remember, basketball is a game and games are meant to be fun. Challenge yourself every day and stay positive and you will be on the fast track to becoming a great shooter.

Becoming a great shooter will require you to learn to shoot the ball correctly, which will be covered in great detail later in this book. But that's the easy part. The difficult part falls on you, the individual, to become aware of adjustments you may need to make and then to take the time and effort to do so. It's going to require a lot of mental toughness, but believe me, you are capable. Just because something hasn't been done before doesn't mean that it can't be done. This is a motto that I live by, and I'm passing it along to you. Keep it etched in the back of your mind as you turn the pages of this book. And finally, always remember, when you are not shooting, someone somewhere else is. How good or how great do you want to become? That is a question only you can answer.

chapter 2

Visualization

Before you take on any endeavor, you must see yourself being successful before you actually perform the task because positive thoughts lead to positive results. This is called visualization. Visualization is the ability to picture yourself performing a task and completing it perfectly. It is an easy thing to do because it does not require any physical training. It is just like daydreaming. However, the mental practice of visualization is something that is all too often overlooked. To become a great shooter, you must incorporate visualization into your routine.

Many athletes use visualization before playing their games to help prepare them for anything that they may encounter during the contest. It also helps build their confidence because they have already seen themselves being successful. When you were a child, you probably often visualized yourself taking the game-winning shot and swishing it. You didn't visualize yourself missing it and failing. Picturing yourself missing a shot is crazy! If you do picture yourself missing shots, then prepare to have all kinds of problems becoming a better shooter. These problems will not be of the physical nature but mental, which in all truth are harder to overcome.

Seeing yourself accomplish something is good for your confidence and self-esteem. Although just visualizing yourself becoming a better shooter will not automatically make you a better shooter, it is a start in the right direction. If you can see, you can do. You must first get your mind, or head, right before you can work on the body and shooting mechanics.

Visualization and the Five Senses

Although we talk about how you should see yourself making shots and succeeding before you actually do so, true visualization requires a more focused degree of concentration. As previously mentioned, visualization is like daydreaming, but not the spacing-out type of daydream. Compare it to the most vivid daydream you've ever experienced, one where you actually see, smell, touch, hear, and even taste the action. Visualization requires you to incorporate those five senses.

Sight

What should you be seeing? Begin with picturing yourself shooting the ball with perfect form. Everything about the shot is perfect. Feet are shoulder-width apart, knees are bent, elbows are tucked in, and the follow-through is crisp. Now see the hoop and more specifically the center of the hoop. This is your target. This is where you want the ball to go. Now see the ball falling through the hoop and swishing through the bottom of the net. You should see each shot almost as if it were a series of photographs arranged in a flip-book. Each shot becomes its own mental movie, and you should actually see frame after frame of yourself hitting shot upon shot. If you can picture it, you can perform it.

Smell

When I suggest that you should engage your sense of smell during visualization, I'm not just talking about conjuring up the salty smell of your own sweat. Incorporating the sense of smell helps you take your photo flip-book and make it more three-dimensional. Now you're not just shooting alone, but there's a defender between you and the basket, and you smell something. It's a very distinct odor, something that leaps off the pictures. It's fear: fear in your opponent, the one obstacle standing in your way. But you know you can take him. Why? Because you smell that fear, and you should become familiar with it. Once you do, you know that there's nothing he can do to stop you from swishing a shot right in his face.

Touch

Let's delve into the senses a little further. Actually feel the ball in your hands. Are you catching a kick-out pass for a knock-down three-pointer? Or are you pulling up for a jump shot off the dribble in transition? No matter the situation, feel the composite leather shell of the ball settle into your shooting pocket and the seams of the ball as you release it from your fingers. Freeze your follow-through, and feel the court beneath your feet as you reconnect with the ground, having just buried yet another jumper.

Hearing

By now, your little photo flip-book should be taking shape. I mean by the time you're through, these images should leap out at you in the same way the scenes from James Cameron's *Avatar* movie does. Now let's add the element of sound. What should you hear? Hear the crowd chanting your name, sure, but don't dismiss the finer sounds. Hear the squeak of your sneakers as you square to the basket and elevate. Hear yourself, calling "swish" as the ball leaves your fingertips. Even hear the actual swish sound as the ball connects with the net. Finally, hear the sound of your defender sighing as you leave him helpless against your uncanny shooting stroke.

Taste

Although you can taste the salt of your own sweat, like smell, it's much more than that. This is the final sense. The culmination of something big. Savor it. Taste it. Taste glory. You shot the ball with perfect form, smelling the fear of your opponent. You felt your feet reconnect with the floor, heard the sound of a swish and the crowd erupting, and tasted the glory. You cannot be stopped. You are a shooter.

Practicing Visualization

If you consistently visualize in such minute detail, you will begin to feel like you are actually shooting the ball. And visualize while saying the word *swish*. Visualization is all about positive mental preparation. Have positive thoughts, see positive thoughts, and even hear positive thoughts. Mental preparation is just as important as physical preparation, and it is especially important on game days. Don't dismiss the visualization process. Great players visualize the entire game. They begin visualizing while driving to the arena. It continues when changing in the locker room and during pregame warm-ups. At halftime, they reassess what needs to happen in the third and fourth quarters, and once again visualize themselves succeeding and pulling out the W. Great players understand that they must train the body, but they must also train the mind.

When first practicing proper visualization, start it in a quiet place where you won't be distracted. You need to give yourself the opportunity to completely concentrate on improving your visualization skills. Don't even think about having music playing or a television on. I know this might be a crazy thought in today's tech-savvy generation, but you might even want to silence your cell phone. You might not catch that witty Facebook status update or Twitter post the second it happens, but trust me, you can always check it later. You need to turn off all these distractions to allow your imagination to be vivid. This is all about creating good visualization habits. Once you can actually see, smell, touch, hear, and taste the action in a quiet place, then you'll be able to bring those skills to the court.

Remember, if you can see, you can do. If you can't see, you can't do. Visualization is such a simple component that is so often overlooked and even taken for granted. The great players visualize. They make time for it and understand the value of being mentally prepared. Failing to prepare is preparing to fail. If you can visualize yourself succeeding, then I guarantee that somewhere inside of you is the capability to succeed. Recognize your potential, and then actualize it.

chapter 3

Shooting Technique

Before you can make a jump shot from the three-point line while on the move, you must be able to make a shot from 2 feet (.6 m) while stationary. The problem is that most players want to go for the shot that is worth the most points. From observing kids at camps and clinics and in pregame warm-ups, it's apparent that the first thing kids want to do no matter how small or big they might be is to get a ball, dribble it to the three-point line, and let it fly. Rarely do I see a youngster come into the gym and start with form shooting. You must be like a baby in your approach to shooting. You crawl, you walk, and then you start to run. It is a process that requires patience and discipline. Just like a little baby, you will stumble and fall, but the key lies in learning to pick yourself up, dust yourself off, and continue on your journey to becoming a better shooter.

This chapter will cover in great detail proper technique for becoming a great shooter. To gain a complete understanding of how to properly shoot a basketball, we will break the shot down into parts. We will cover foot positioning, body positioning, how to hold the ball, how to release the ball, and where to target your shot. At the end of the chapter is an evaluation checklist, making it easy for you to identify where your problem areas may be. Pay careful attention to the details provided throughout and honestly evaluate your own technique. The greatest shooters are constantly critiquing their own form. You should do the same.

Stance

When shooting, you build the shot from the ground up, just like building a house. In this case, the foot position for shooting the ball is your foundation and should be the same for all shots, whether shooting a jumper or a free shot or shooting from beyond the three-point line. Consistency leads to greatness and consistency starts with the feet.

To begin, start with your feet together (see figure 3.1*a*) and slide the foot opposite the shooting side, for a right-handed shooter this is the left foot, back until the toes are even with the arch of the shooting foot (see figure 3.1*b*). Then, space the feet so that they are shoulder-width apart (see figure 3.1*c*). This will ensure that the base isn't too narrow or too wide. If you have a narrow base, you will have poor balance and it will hinder the range of your shot (see figure 3.2*a*). If your base is too wide, you won't have the quickness or explosiveness necessary to get your shot off successfully (see figure 3.2*b*). In this stance, the lead foot, or shooting foot, is the foot on the same side that you shoot the ball with. For a right-handed shooter, this is the right foot. The toes of the lead foot point toward the target. This positioning creates the *shot line*,

FIGURE 3.1   Assuming the proper shooting stance.

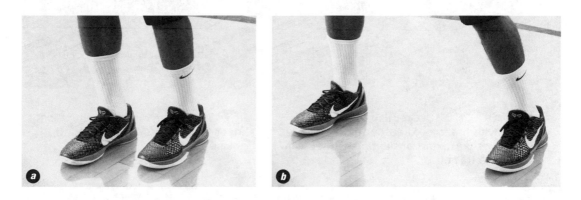

FIGURE 3.2   A stance that is *(a)* too narrow and *(b)* too wide.

in which the toe, knee, hip, elbow, shoulder, wrist, and basketball are situated as close to a straight line as possible in relation to the target (see figure 3.3). Maintaining this line will increase your shooting percentage and eliminate unnecessary movements throughout your shooting motion. This is the stance you should assume for all of your shots.

Once the feet are shoulder-width apart and positioned properly, you must ensure that your knees are bent so that you have better balance, more power, and more explosiveness in the shot. When you bend your knees, you should also bend slightly at the hips, bringing your head down so that the shoulders are positioned in front of the feet and the head in front of the shoulders (see figure 3.4). If you just bend at the knees and don't bring the head and shoulders forward, your heels will stay on the floor, forcing you off balance when you catch the ball and start your shooting motion.

FIGURE 3.3 Creating the *shot line* with the toes, knee, hip, elbow, shoulder, wrist, and basketball aligned with the target.

FIGURE 3.4 Bending at the hips and knees for increased balance and power.

Many shooters will bend at the knees but fail to bend at the hips, making the body too upright and leaving the heels nailed to the floor. To practice bending at the hips, lean forward and attempt to get as close to the basket as you can without moving the feet. To do this, you will naturally be forced to bend at the hips. Hold this position for a few seconds and repeat several times to become familiar with how the positioning feels.

Arms

With an understanding of stance and body positioning in place, we now transition to the arms. While your legs and core body muscles serve as the power source for your shot, your arms, wrists, and fingers take on more of a finesse role. They control your touch and where you shoot the ball. We will also explore finer elements that dictate how the ball will release off your fingertips. We will now discuss the shooting hand and how you should grip the ball, as well as elbow positioning and how to properly set your balance hand to maximize shot accuracy.

Shooting Hand

Your shooting hand, the right hand if you are right handed and the left hand if you're left handed, should be in the center of the ball in order to balance and control the ball during the shot. To do this, position the shooting hand with the palm facing the sky or ceiling and place the ball into the hand (see figure 3.5). The ball rests on your fingertips and fingerpads. The palm does not touch the ball. This ensures that you can put proper rotation or backspin on the ball when you shoot it. Putting your palm on the ball forces the ball to roll off the hand. No matter

how big or small your hand, the ball will balance easily on the fingertips and fingerpads if your hand is in the correct position in the center of the ball. Now bring the ball back toward the head to form the letter L with the shooting arm (see figure 3.6). Make sure that you see a little bit of daylight between your shooting hand and the ball. A good way to check to see if there is enough daylight, or space, is to place two fingers from your nonshooting hand between the heel of your shooting hand and the basketball (see figure 3.7). This technique will assure complete and total ball control as you position yourselves to shoot.

FIGURE 3.5 **Proper grip on a basketball when preparing to shoot.**

FIGURE 3.6 **L-shaped position of the shooting arm when preparing to shoot.**

FIGURE 3.7 **Checking the space between the shooting hand and the ball.**

FIGURE 3.8   **Seaming the basketball when preparing to shoot.**

Once you find the proper hand position, you need to make sure that you position the ball in the shooting hand the same way every time. Some say that the ball's position doesn't matter because the ball is round, but it is evident that great shooters *seam* the basketball. In other words, they always have beautiful rotation on their shots because of the way they grip the ball. You should find the valve, or air hole, and place that between your index finger and middle finger (see figure 3.8). Now your shooting hand is in the center of the ball, and the ball is seamed the correct way as well. The more you practice seaming the ball, the easier it will become, and eventually you will be able to feel the seams without looking at them.

Elbow

Believe it or not, the elbow is the single most important component in your ability to make shots consistently. The most common flaw is the elbow sticking out during the shot (see figure 3.9). Some coaches refer to this problem as the *chicken wing* problem because of the way the shooter's elbow looks like a chicken's wing sticking out from the body. If the elbow is sticking out, it diminishes the shooter's chances of being able to make shots because it is not in alignment with the target, and the shooter is unable to get the ball in the air with the proper arch. Proper positioning of the elbow helps keep the ball straight and allows for full extension on the follow-through, which is discussed later.

When the elbow is in the L-shaped position, as discussed previously, the shot should be consistently straight if you are in proper alignment. Once the shooting arm is in the L-shaped position, you should make sure that the

FIGURE 3.9   **Elbow sticks out, creating a chicken wing.**

elbow is directly under the ball and above the shooting foot (see figure 3.10). This L-shaped positioning is key. If you bend the shooting elbow too much and distort the L, you won't be shooting the ball; you will be slinging the ball. Conversely, if you don't bend the elbow enough, you will be pushing the ball. By maintaining the L-shape, you will properly lift the ball. Be a *lifter*, not a *slinger* or a *pusher*. When the elbow is in alignment, it will face directly at the target. Your wrist should be cocked and locked with the basketball properly gripped. Make sure to bend the wrist back until the skin wrinkles.

When your elbow is properly positioned, theoretically, you should only miss long or short shots. This leaves only a handful of other slight adjustments you may need to consider. These adjustments

FIGURE 3.10 **Proper position for the shooting-arm elbow when preparing to shoot.**

are typically things like ensuring that you finish the follow-through with the elbow fully extended or ensuring that you finish the shot with the elbow above the eyebrow. If your elbow sticks out, you will likely miss the shot to the left or right of the target. This is an alignment problem, which is ultimately more difficult to correct than the other types of adjustments.

There are a few reasons that so many players shoot with their elbow out. First, when young kids start shooting a basketball, they typically shoot at a 10-foot (3 m) basket, forcing them to throw the ball rather than shoot it. They practice incorrectly because of the conditions. This allows bad habits to develop, which become more difficult to break with age. Second, many players do a poor job of being *shot ready* when receiving a pass. Being shot ready refers to the idea that a player should be prepared to shoot before even receiving a pass. To be shot ready, a player shows the palm of the shooting hand to the passer, and the elbow is already in an L-shaped position and the wrist is already wrinkled. From this L-shaped position, all the player needs to do is catch the ball (see figure 3.11a) and lift the arm into shooting position (see figure 3.11b). The elbow is aligned above the shooting foot before the player even catches the ball. It remains aligned on the catch-and-lift and extends straight on the finished follow-through.

A final reason players struggle with the chicken wing elbow is because they don't spend enough time practicing their form for one-handed shooting. When practicing one-handed shooting, the key is to position the elbow correctly or the ball will fall off the hand.

FIGURE 3.11 Catching the ball in *(a)* a shot-ready position and *(b)* lifting to shoot.

Shooting-Hand Form Shooting

This drill is used to help players perfect their alignment, using the techniques we have discussed so far. To practice shooting-hand form shooting, assume the proper shooting stance, and grip the ball in your shooting hand with the wrist wrinkled and the elbow in the L-shaped position. You will not need your balance hand for this drill. Oftentimes, the balance hand is the main culprit for creating the chicken wing elbow. A player might move the ball out of alignment and toward the balance hand, causing the shooting elbow to pop out, resulting in a poor release.

In this drill, we take the balance hand out of the equation, forcing the shooter to maintain proper positioning of the shooting arm and elbow. Beginning directly in front of the basket, start 2 feet (.6 m) from the rim and shoot until you make five shots. Then take a half step back and shoot until you make five more shots. Continue to move back until your form breaks down—that is, when you are no longer shooting the ball, but appear to be throwing it instead. Once your form breaks down, you have reached the limit of you shooting range.

To shoot a high percentage, you would be ill advised to attempt shots from beyond this distance because your technique will be compromised. As you mature and become stronger, you will be able to extend your range. The goal is to work your way back until you've shot from 10 spots, adding up your makes until they total 50. To keep one-handed form shooting interesting, you can change the angle that you shoot from. For example, instead of working a straight-on shot, you could work one particular side out toward the wing. You could also work your way back along the baseline.

Another method for warming up with one-handed form shooting is shooting *around the world* style. Start directly in front of the rim and make your usual five. After that, step out to the side along the first lane marker, just above the box. Make five more, and then go to the other side. Continue your way up the lane along each side. When you've reached the free-throw line (or what I call the free-shot line), make five more, and then continue to work your way back until your form breaks down.

Another effective way to practice one-handed form shooting is to shoot *strings* style, in which you go for a certain number in a row or shoot until you miss. This requires more concentration, but sometimes it helps shooters buckle down and focus because the typical routine of making five before advancing can become monotonous and not present much of a challenge. Understand that one-handed form shooting is a fundamental drill that shooters use even at the highest level of competition. Before you get into a more rigorous shooting workout, begin by practicing this drill from a variety of angles, working your way back a half step at a time and making it a staple of your daily routine.

Balance Hand

After you have assumed the proper stance and position of your shooting hand, you should add the balance hand to the mix. The primary function of the balance hand is to help balance the ball and to lift it. It does *not* shoot the ball or guide the ball. You may hear a lot of coaches refer to the balance hand as a guide hand, but that terminology implies that the hand guides the ball into the basket, which is incorrect. I've also heard other coaches use the terms off-hand or nonshooting hand. Such negative terminology shouldn't be used when referring to this hand. The term *nonshooter*, for example, would imply that you cannot shoot, which isn't the message that we want to send. Great teaching involves reinforcing positive thoughts whenever possible because positive thoughts lead to positive actions.

The balance hand is properly placed along the side of the ball. To ensure that the balance hand's palm does not touch the ball, rest the ball on the fingertips and fingerpads, just like you would for the shooting hand.

FIGURE 3.12 **T-shaped position of the shooting and balance-hand thumbs when preparing to shoot.**

To find the proper position, if the thumbs were to come together, they would form a letter "T," with the balance hand thumb forming the top of the letter T (see figure 3.12).

Placing the balance hand on the side of the ball allows the shooter to be able to see the target with both eyes. It also eliminates potential side-to-side motion as the ball is lifted. Eliminating motion increases accuracy. A common mistake of young players is placing the balance hand in front of the ball, which is incorrect (see figure 3.13*a*). This placement blocks the target and perhaps a defender from the shooter's view. Another common mistake is placing the balance hand on top of

FIGURE 3.13 **Mistakenly placing the balance hand (*a*) in front of the ball and (*b*) on top of the ball.**

the ball, as shown in figure 3.13*b*, which forces the shooter to release that hand at some point before shooting. This adds too much movement and also adds time to the shot. It's crucial that players be efficient with their movement so they can develop a quick release. In addition to these issues, some players actually develop the bad habit of moving the shooting hand to the side of the ball when they add the balance hand. The shooting hand must always stay under the ball and in the center of the ball. If the shooter moves the shooting hand, he or she ends up shooting with two hands, or the balance hand becomes inadvertently involved with the shot.

Balance-Hand Form Shooting

This drill is a continuation of drill for shooting-hand form shooting. We're now adding the balance hand to the equation. Where shooting-hand form shooting focuses on perfecting alignment, balance-hand form shooting is about maintaining that alignment when the balance hand comes into play. To perform this drill, shooters start 2 feet (.6 m) from the basket and place their balance hand on the side of the ball when their shooting arm is in the L-shaped position. Shooters must remember to keep the arm straight by keeping the elbow in and the hand under the center of the ball. Shooters assume the proper positioning, and before they take a shot, a partner or coach checks the positioning of their shooting and balance arms. Shooters make five shots and take half a step back and make five more shots. As with shooting-hand form shooting, this continues until the shooters' form breaks down. Players take the same approach with balance-hand form shooting as they do with shooting-hand form shooting. The goal is to make five shots from 10 spots, whether it's straight on, at an angle or around-the-world style. When shooters find that they have mastered the traditional make-five style, shoot in strings, either for a specific number of shots in a row or until a miss.

Hitting the Target

If you are to become a consistent shooter, you must have a consistent target. More often than not, if coaches were to ask their team what they look at when they shoot, they would hear different answers. Some players may say the front of the basket, others the back of the basket. Some would say the hooks that hold the net in place or that they just don't know. A select few might say the center of the basket.

The center of the basket is always the target that a shooter should focus on, no matter where the player shoots from on the court. Players who do not look at the center of the basket will not become as great at shooting as they could. If shooters focus on the front of the rim from straight on, for example, what would they focus on when shooting a jump shot from the corner? They would not look at the front of the rim because they could no longer see the front of the rim. The target changes and so does a player's consistency, but the center of the basket is always the center of the basket, no matter where the player shoots from. Consistent target, consistent shooter. It may take more concentration to focus on the center of the basket, but to become better shooters, players need to have better concentration and focus anyway. Shooters should learn that their main objective is to keep their eyes on the target and never to follow the flight of the ball.

Now, the argument that I hear most in regards to targeting the center of the basket is that a shooter can't see an actual spot when aiming for the center of the basket. Because this is true, the shooter should focus on putting the ball somewhere in the middle of that large space otherwise known as the hoop. Aiming for the center of the hoop allows a little room for error, meaning that a shooter can actually shoot slightly long or short, left or right, or a combination and still make a successful shot.

Note, however, that there is one case where the shooter's target will change and this is when shooting a bank shot off the backboard. In this case, the target is no longer the center of the basket, but instead is the top corner of the small square on the backboard that is closest to the shooter. This will be covered in more detail in chapter 7.

Follow-Through

The follow-through is the last part of the shot. Understanding the nuances of the follow-through is a great tool for giving feedback regarding what was done correctly or what may have been done incorrectly. The follow-through also provides the last bit of positive power and energy to the shot.

To follow through correctly, after the ball is released, the shooting arm is fully extended with the elbow above the eyebrow and slightly in front of the body. It should stay in the *shot line*: the toe, knee, hip, shoulder, elbow, wrist, and hand all maintaining alignment. The shooting arm should not finish across the shooter's face or go outside of the shoulder. For a right-handed shooter, the right hand stays on the right side of the body and the left hand stays on the left side of the body. The shooting hand should be pointed straight toward the target and in the hoop with fingers pointed down at about a 45-degree angle toward the floor (pretend you are putting your hand in a cookie jar!), with the wrist becoming the highest point of the shooting arm (see figure 3.14). The balance hand should also be up in the air after the release. Too many players drop the balance hand, and this throws their shot off, creating a power struggle in which half of the body is trying to go toward the target on the shooting side, and the balance hand is pulling the other side away from the target (see figure 3.15). The body twists and turns

FIGURE 3.14 **A follow-through after the ball is released.**

FIGURE 3.15 **Improperly dropping the balance hand at follow-through.**

and no longer finishes straight. The shooter must hold the hands high on the follow-through. The shooter's head remains still in the center of the body with the eyes focused on the target not on following the flight of the ball.

When you release the ball, you should *freeze* the finish until the ball has swished through the bottom of the net. Many players tend to drop their arms too soon, preventing the coach from getting feedback on the shot before assessing the player's body position. Was the elbow above the eyebrow? Was the hand in the hoop? Was the finish straight? Get in the habit of freezing your follow-through in practice so that your coach can provide you with valuable feedback. If you drop your hands too quickly in practice, you will drop them even more quickly in a game because things happen much more quickly in games.

Freeze Follow-Through

To help shooters learn to freeze their follow-through, you can overemphasize the position with their hands held high. To perform this drill, have shooters take shots within their shooting range and have them freeze the follow-through position until the ball hits the floor. Check to make sure that both hands are held high and that the shooting arm finishes in the shot line. Incorporate this drill into your shooting warm-up along with one-handed form shooting and two-handed form shooting.

Eggs on the Rim

This practice drill is used to help shooters perfect their follow-through by getting more arch on their shot and staying off the rim. This is also directly related to targeting the center of the basket. To perform this drill, the shooter assumes a standard shooting stance and standard shooting-arm and balance-arm position. The shooter visualizes eggs standing upright on the rim. The goal of the drill is simple: Don't break the eggs. This drill will accomplish two things. First, it will force the shooter to strive for perfect follow-through with the elbow above the eyebrow and the hand in the hand-in-the-hoop position, allowing for maximum arch on the shot. Second, it will strengthen the shooter's visual focus. Shooters will get in the habit of swishing shots because they don't want to break any eggs. The ones that rattle in will frustrate them. But you know what? They still made the shot.

Shot Technique Evaluation

In this section, you will find an evaluation checklist to help you critique your shooting form (see figure 3.16). Why are you missing shots? Are you bending at the knees but not at your hips? Is your elbow under the ball, or do you have a chicken wing? These are just a few sample questions that you can ask yourself as you go through this list. You may find that you have one major area of concern. For example, let's say your balance hand is positioned on the top of the ball. Tackle that issue first, and correct it. Once it's fixed, you may realize that your body balance could be better, so you adjust your feet.

FIGURE 3.16   Shot Technique Evaluation Checklist

	Key points	Rating	Notes
Stance	▪ Staggered stance (toes even with arch) ▪ Feet shoulder-width apart ▪ Toe to target ▪ Knees and hips bent ▪ Heels off the floor	____Never ____Sometimes ____Most of the time ____Every time	
Shooting hand, arm, and elbow	▪ Basketball seamed ▪ Elbow L-shaped directly under the ball ▪ Wrist wrinkled ▪ Daylight between the ball and palm	____Never ____Sometimes ____Most of the time ____Every time	
Balance hand and arm	▪ Placed on the side ▪ Daylight grip ▪ Thumbs make a T	____Never ____Sometimes ____Most of the time ____Every time	
Release and follow-through	▪ Elbow above eyebrow ▪ Shot line maintained ▪ Shooting hand goose-necked ▪ Balance hand up, straight	____Never ____Sometimes ____Most of the time ____Every time	

From D. Hopla, 2012, *Basketball shooting* (Champaign, IL: Human Kinetics).

Take it in stages. Even elite shooters constantly evaluate their technique. Ray Allen might swish five NBA threes in a row, but then clang the sixth. What happened? Did he freeze his follow-through? Was he toe to target? Chances are, Ray will evaluate that miss, make the adjustment, and then nail that next long ball.

This checklist is all about evaluating your habits in terms of consistency. To be a great shooter, you must become consistent. Be honest with your evaluation, and involve your coaches. Go through each element and assess yourself. Once you have an idea of where you think you need improvement, take that information to your coaches and get their feedback. Don't think of the process as being critical of yourself in a negative light. This is all about improving and getting better. Everyone starts somewhere, and this checklist provides a framework for you to work from. Take advantage of it and the resources around you, and you will be on your way to becoming a great shooter.

You now possess the knowledge to correctly shoot the basketball. Shooting is a craft that must be honed. Understand that consistency is perhaps the single most important factor in determining your success as a shooter. Not only consistency within the fundamental breakdown of your technique, but also consistency as you vary your practice routines. For example, as you go through this book, you will discover the different methods for receiving the ball and for correctly placing the ball in your shot pocket whether you are shooting off a pass or off of a dribble. No matter the style of shot, the shooting technique itself will be consistent with the elements covered in this chapter. The shot technique evaluation checklist is not merely a guideline for you to use to evaluate what you do or don't do in regards to your technique. It's also a checklist, a step-by-step way to evaluate your shot so that you can be consistent as you develop different facets of your game. How good or great do you intend to become? Much of that will depend on how consistent you are with your shooting technique.

Free Shots

ow that you have your shooting fundamentals down, you must be able to shoot a free shot, or one-point shot. This is also referred to by many as the foul shot or free throw. I do not like to call it a foul shot or a free throw because *foul* is a negative word, and *throw* creates a negative image. You must always be positive in your thoughts, actions, and words. If something is foul, that means it is stinking, rotten, nasty, and no good. Do you want to be a stinking, rotten, nasty, no-good shooter? Of course not, but many are. Then there's the term *free throw*. You do not want to throw the ball. You want to shoot a basketball, not throw it. You throw a football and a baseball, but you shoot a basketball. If you want to be great, you have to think correctly. *Free shots* fall in line with this train of thought, and to be a great player, your thoughts must be different from other people's thoughts.

When shooting free shots, do not settle for mediocrity. There is no excuse for you to make less than 80 percent of your free-shot attempts. It seems that most everyone has accepted mediocrity from the one-point line. Listen to game announcers, for example. They will often refer to a specific player as an excellent *foul shooter*, and in the very next breath say that the player makes 75 percent of his or her shots. When did 75 percent become excellent? To increase your free-shot percentage, you must first visualize yourself shooting the ball and swishing it, as discussed in chapter 2, and then you must practice shooting using correct shooting technique, as discussed in chapter 3. Successful free-shot shooting comes down to this: perfect practice makes perfect.

The problem that a lot of players have on all levels is that they do not have a solid, sound routine that they stick to when shooting from the charity stripe. They may bounce the ball one time before the first shot and then miss; then on the second shot they decide to try something different and bounce it three times. They may line up a step or two away from the line instead of on the line, or they may be a step to the left or a step to the right. They may not position their fingers along the seams of the ball, resulting in a different grip with every shot. Shooting from the line is all about consistency, and in order to be consistent and develop muscle memory, you must do the same thing over and over and over.

Throughout the history of the game there have always been great free-shot shooters such as Bill Sharman, Rick Barry, Calvin Murphy, Mark Price, Reggie Miller, Steve Nash, Ray Allen, Chauncey Billups, and Rip Hamilton. Rick Barry shot the ball underhanded and was an excellent free-shot shooter. His technique is testimony to the fact that if you practice something enough you can be very successful at it. But you must put the time in and do the repetitions. On the other hand, there are also plenty of *foul shooters* who have left their mark on the history of the game. Here are some famous foul shooters: Wilt Chamberlain, Shaquille O'Neal, Ben Wallace, Dennis Rodman, and Dwight Howard.

Remember this: when you are an excellent shooter, everyone is shocked when you miss. But when you are a *foul shooter*, everyone is shocked when you make one.

Free-Shot Technique

Free shots will involve the same fundamental shooting techniques that we discussed in chapter 3. We take you through the physical components as well as the mental components of the free shot. The technique you use for free shots is virtually identical to the technique you would use when practicing the drill for balance-hand shooting form. The major difference with free shots is the mental component of being on stage or on the spot. Recall the importance of being consistent. If you are consistent with how you shoot the ball, then you can develop a sense of confidence when you step to the line.

Stance

Great shooters attempt to align their feet in the exact spot every time they shoot. When stepping to the one-point line for a pair of *free shots*, obtaining proper stance becomes much easier than, say, coming off a

How Many Shots Should You Take?

Far too often, players will practice all kinds of fancy dribbling moves that they will never use in a game, but they won't put the time in at the line. So exactly how many free shots should a player take every day that they shoot? You need to be more interested in makes than takes. A lot of coaches end practice with "foul" shooting. They ask players to shoot 50 and go home. In this situation, a poor shooter will most likely shoot 50 as quickly as possible so he or she can get out of the gym and go home. Practicing that way is almost like giving someone a machine gun. He or she might get 50 rounds off quickly, but not many shots will have hit the target. Instead, a coach who asks players to make 50 before going home requires more focus and concentration from players. Eventually, the players who want to be great will aim to make 100 free shots before heading home. And guess what! It doesn't take long to make 100 free shots—perhaps anywhere from 20 to 30 minutes if you are a good shooter and depending on the number of bounces that you like to use.

FIGURE 4.1 **Position of the shooting foot for a free shot for a right-handed shooter.**

screen for a jump shot. This is because free shots are stationary shots, allowing players to properly align their feet using the mechanics discussed in chapter 3. Yet another aspect of free shots is the tack or nail located in the center of most one-point lines. The first thing you should do is locate this tack or nail. This spot is aligned with the center of the basket. In the rare event that you find yourself shooting at a line with no tack or nail, do your best to determine where the center of the basket is and place your shooting foot there (right foot if you are right-handed). A majority of courts should have a tack or nail in place, so this shouldn't be an issue.

If you are a right-handed shooter, you would align your right foot with the tack, as shown in figure 4.1. If you are left handed, you would do just the opposite and align with your left foot. This positioning sets you up to shoot the ball in your shot line in accordance with your shooting hand.

Once the shooting foot is aligned, place the other foot next to the shooting foot (see figure 4.2a) and slide it back until the toes are even with the arch of the shooting foot (see figure 4.2b). Next, move the back foot (nonshooting foot) over until the feet are shoulder-width apart (see figure 4.2c). You are now in a staggered stance, obtaining perfect balance.

FIGURE 4.2 **Assuming the proper free-shot shooting stance.**

Once the feet are set, bend at the hips and knees to generate power and momentum for the free shot. When bending at the hips, bring the head and shoulders down or forward so that the shoulders are in front of the feet and the head is in front of the shoulders. Then, bend at the knees until the heels come off the floor (see figure 4.3). Bending at the hips and knees gives you proper balance and power to get the ball to the basket.

If you're a younger player, you might need to bend at the hips and knees slightly more in order to generate enough power to get the ball to the basket. If you still require additional power, you might consider stepping into the free shot. To do this, first establish your stance exactly as described previously, and then bring the shooting foot behind the nonshooting foot. When ready to shoot, take the shooting foot and step to the tack or nail. This step

FIGURE 4.3 **With the hips and knees bent, you are balanced and have adequate power to shoot.**

allows younger players to gather enough power to ensure that the ball will reach the basket. However, you must be cautious of stepping over the line when using this technique because that will result in a violation and a forfeiture of the free shot. What is truly important is to stress the bend at both the knees and the hips. As a younger player, if you bend just at the knees and do not bend at the hips, you will fail to bring the head and shoulders forward. This means that the heels will likely remain in contact with the floor and you will be flat footed until you raise the ball. If you shoot in this fashion you will have significantly less power, and your free-shot attempts will likely clang off the front of the rim.

Establishing a Routine for Free Shots

If you want to be an excellent free-shot shooter, you must develop a routine that you are comfortable with. Let's stress that the details of the actual routine are inconsequential. What's important is that you be consistent—both with the routine you use in practice as well as the routine you use in games. The routine never changes. Remember, successful free-shot shooting comes down to this: perfect practice makes perfect. In developing your routine, you should take several factors into consideration:

▶ **How many bounces are you going to use?** For example, some players like to bounce the ball one time, others three times. Again, it doesn't matter how many times you bounce the ball before shooting the one-point shot. What's important is that you use the same number of bounces every time.

▶ **What is your thought process before shooting the ball?** Are you flustered that you missed the layup before the shot, thus missing your opportunity for the old-fashioned three-point play? Did you miss your two previous free-shot attempts? Whatever negative thoughts might be rambling around in your brain, don't bring them to the line. The only thing that you should be focused on is that next free shot.

▶ **Are you visualizing yourself swishing the basketball?** In today's NBA, nobody does a better job visualizing their shot than Steve Nash. Every time he steps to the line and before the referee has even handed him the ball, he practices his shot mechanics, and you can see it in his eyes: swish, swish. He's making these shots. He visualizes himself succeeding. You should do the same.

▶ **Are you relaxed?** Take a breath. Competition is exhilarating, and often-times a player can tense up. Take a breath and learn to relax at the line. It will make you a more focused and consistent free-shot shooter.

▶ **Do you act as though you own your routine?** What I mean by this is that in addition to the number of bounces that you choose to use, you can incorporate other rituals to personalize or own your routine. For example, Jason Kidd blows a kiss to the basket before shooting his free shots. Hall of famer Karl Malone used to talk a complete blue streak to himself before every shot attempt. Whatever you choose to do, own it and be consistent.

Arms

Once your feet are set, you must have a proper grip on the basketball. No matter the size of the shooting hand, it should be under and in the center of the basketball and on the seams, as described in chapter 3. The ball should rest on the fingertips and fingerpads, without the palm touching the ball. You should have a comfortable, firm grip on the ball, with the fingers not too wide or too close together. The balance hand should be on the side of the ball so that the thumbs of both hands form the letter T. The palm of the balance hand does not touch the ball, either—only the fingertips and fingerpads. The function of the balance hand is to steady the ball and help lift it during the shot. See figure 4.4 for an example of the proper grip.

Once the balance hand is placed, the wrist of the shooting hand should be wrinkled, cocked, and locked. The elbow of the shooting hand is tucked in and aligned directly above the shooting foot so that the shooting arm forms the letter L. You have

FIGURE 4.4   **Note the space between the palm of the shooting hand and the ball. Also note the letter T created by the positioning of the thumbs and the letter L formed by the shooting arm.**

now created the fully loaded *shot line*, where the toe, knee, hip, elbow, shoulder, wrist, and ball are in alignment with the center of the basket.

If you are flat-footed on the free shot, you will have negative motion. Once you raise the ball, all of the weight will be back on the heels, resulting in a negative motion. By negative motion, I mean that the body weight will move backward instead of forward. This is negated as the heels come off the floor with the knees and hips extending upward with the body. *Bend and extend* is a catchphrase that illustrates the rhythm you should practice when rising up to shoot the ball.

FIGURE 4.5 **Freezing the follow-through.**

Follow-Through

On the follow-through, you should remain up on the toes or balls of the feet until the ball swishes cleanly through the bottom of the net. The shooting arm should be fully extended with the elbow finishing above the eyebrow and the hand into the hoop (see figure 4.5). The balance hand remains up; it does not drop on the shot. Freeze the follow-through until the shot swishes through the bottom of the net. If you do not hold the follow-through and drop the arms too early, you most likely won't be able to stay up on the toes, either, causing the shot to either fall short or off to the left or right.

Free-Shot Drills

There are countless ways to drill your free-shot shooting and keep things interesting. Getting your 50 or 100 makes at practice is an essential step that any player must take to become a great free-shot shooter, but even I understand as both a player and a coach that those repetitions can sometimes become mundane. Here are a few competitive free-shot shooting drills to help keep you focused on improving this crucial and game-changing skill.

Swish

This is a great drill for getting players to take pride in free-shot shooting. Players are paired up at a basket. One player shoots two free shots and then the next player shoots two. Players get two points for a swish and one point for a make. If the ball does not go in, one point is deducted from the player's score. Play to 11 points, and you must win by two.

3-25 Drill

The goal of this drill is to make 25 free shots before getting three misses. To accomplish this, you must shoot close to 90 percent. You can perform this drill individually, or it can be a practice-ending drill for the whole team. When the whole team is involved, you can add pressure by running sprints. For the full team, each player shoots two shots. The team must make 25 shots before missing three. Every shot that does not go in results in a sprint up the court and back before the drill continues. Ending practice with this drill is a real test of mental toughness, but it encourages camaraderie among team members and helps to build trust between the players and coaches as each shooter steps to the line.

Five Free Shots, Five Balance-Hand Layups

Oftentimes, you can economize practice time by working on other skills without players' realizing it. This drill does just that. You shoot a free shot and freeze the follow-through, waiting until the ball hits the floor. Then attack the rim and go in for a layup with the balance hand. Then dribble back to the line hard with the balance hand. This drill works on three skills at once. It emphasizes shooting free shots while fatigued, shooting balance-hand layups, and improving ball handling with the balance hand.

Make Two, Sprint to Baseline

This is a great drill for conditioning yourself to making two consecutive free shots. In this drill, the goal is to make two shots and then sprint to the opposite baseline before returning to make two more. Repeat this until you have made 20 shots. If you miss a shot, immediately sprint down and back. You don't want to get in the habit of shooting one for two at the line. This drill requires concentration, and the periodic sprinting keeps it gamelike. After all, you are likely to be winded when you step to the line in a game. This drill simulates shooting under those conditions.

Free shots are a major part of the game that far too many players overlook. Don't believe me? Just check the box scores on any given day and I guarantee you that the point differential in virtually any game could have been made up if teams had made their free shots. A classic example of missed free-shot opportunities occurred in the 2008 NCAA Championship game when Memphis clanged four off the rim within the final two minutes of regulation, failing to extend their lead and eventually losing to Kansas in overtime. One of those free shots was missed by none other than the NBA's 2011 MVP Derrick Rose. I think it's safe to say he found himself a *foul shooter* at a most inconvenient moment. The real secret to mastering free shots is to shoot more of them. Remember, when you aren't out there practicing, someone somewhere else is. When you meet that person, and the game is on the line, who will be ready to step up to the line and ice the game?

chapter 5

Midrange Jump Shots

A midrange jump shot is a shot taken inside the three-point arc, but outside of the painted area dominated by larger low-post players. In this chapter, we cover the easiest type of jump shot—the straight-on midrange jump shot.

Midrange shots must be made consistently because they are essential in developing your shooting stroke. Once you master the midrange jump shot, it will open up the rest of your game. Don't believe me? Look no further than Michael Jordan, winner of more scoring titles, 10 total, than any other player in NBA history. Most people think of Michael as a high-flying dunker. Although it's true that many of his points were found above the rim, Michael Jordan led the league in scoring all of those years because he was able to hit the 15-foot (4.5 m) jump shot. This shot makes you unguardable. Think about what goes through a defender's mind when you hit that shot. Will he or she play up on you? Boom! You have a lane to the basket. Michael knew this and used it to his advantage better than any other player in the history of the sport.

The problem that most players have is wanting to go out to the three-point line before being able to consistently hit an open 12- to 15-foot (3.6-4.5 m) jump shot. Start in close and work your way out just like you did with your form shooting. You must be able to make an open 10-footer (3 m) before you can make an open 20-footer (6 m). Michael understood this as well, and you can see that later in his career he became a much improved long-range shooter. However, it all started by his first mastering this midrange weapon.

Technique for Midrange Jump Shots

The shooting mechanics of the midrange jump shot rely on the details discussed in chapter 3. The major difference is that you will shoot this shot in the air: *jump* shot. We will explore fundamental techniques for shooting this shot as a straight-on shot both off the catch and as a pull-up shot off the dribble.

The straight-on jump shot is one of the easiest shots to teach and the shot most common to players. It is the shot that everyone practices the most because it requires a minimal amount of movement, making it is the easiest to practice. For this shot, players do not move from side to side or shoot off the dribble. In the straight-on jump shot, the ball comes to you from an inside-out pass. You can practice this with a teammate standing under the rim, passing the ball out to you, or you can easily simulate a pass to yourself by performing a *spinout*. A spinout simply means that you toss the ball out in front of yourself and put some spin on it so it rotates toward you. When the ball bounces off the floor, it will come back at you, thus simulating a pass. When shooting the straight-on jump shot, the basic mechanics never change: simply take a one-two step into the shot. A right-handed shooter steps with the left foot first and then brings the right foot into shooting position.

Stance

Before receiving the ball, you should assume a balanced, athletic stance with the feet shoulder-width apart and with the knees bent. When bending the knees, you should also bend at the hips, bringing the head and shoulders forward. The shoulders should be in front of the feet and the head in front of the shoulders. When in the proper position, your heels lift off the floor, putting you on your toes. Note that this athletic stance is a fundamental position in basketball. You assume this position if you are preparing to catch a pass, slide defensively, or box out and rebound. In this instance, you are now prepared to step forward to receive the ball for your straight-on jump shot.

Receiving the Ball

Before you step to receive the ball, you must show a *target* to your teammate who has the ball. This helps the teammate understand where you want the ball. To show a target, the palm of the shooting hand points to the passer with the wrist wrinkled back, cocked and locked, the fingertips pointing to the ceiling, and the elbow locked in an L-shaped position. We call this *palm to passer*. The fingertips of the balance hand should point to the passer. The passer should see only the palm of the shooting hand, not the palm of the balance hand. This position forms what is called the *shot pocket* (see figure 5.1). Note that if you ensure that only the palm of the shooting hand is facing the passer, you will never stick your elbow out, enabling you to maintain the proper *shot line*, as discussed in chapter 3 (page 18).

FIGURE 5.1   **Forming a *shot pocket* in order to give a passer a target to pass to.**

As the ball comes toward you, begin your one-two step. The first step is all about catching the ball with your pivot foot established. You should move forward to meet the ball using a long step. A right-handed player would step with the left foot and a left-handed player would step with the right foot. A long aggressive step into the shot helps you get to the ball quicker and helps you stay low. This step should be done with the heel hitting the floor first, as shown in figure 5.2*a*, then transferring the weight onto the toes or the ball of the foot, as shown in figure 5.2*b*. This foot has now become your pivot foot.

Time the catching phase of the straight-on jump shot so that you catch the ball as you establish your pivot foot. You should keep your eyes on the ball and catch it with both hands, watching it all the way into the shot pocket. With the ball caught, immediately sight the target, which is the center of the basket. Now, the *two* of the one-two step should already be in motion. Do not catch and pause. Bring your shooting foot forward so that you are in your original athletic stance, bending at the knees and hips. Again, don't pause. Elevate off the ground into your shooting motion. Be the aggressor. The one-two step allows you to gain momentum and bring your legs into the shot in an efficient and balanced manner.

FIGURE 5.2   **Stepping to the ball during the pass using a one-two step.**

Calling the Ball

You should always call for the ball to let your teammates know that you are open and ready to receive the pass. Calling involves much more than just shouting for the basketball. Great shooters call for the ball with their mouths and eyes and by showing hand targets. Calling for the ball will help you catch the ball in rhythm so that you are prepared to shoot because you have alerted the passer that you are open, and you are encouraging him or her to deliver a better pass.

Here are a few things to keep in mind when calling the ball:

▶ **Demand the ball.** You should be loud. If you quietly say "ball" in a packed gymnasium, the only one who will know you are open and ready to shoot will be you. Demand the ball, "Ball, ball, ball, ball, ball!"

▶ **Use your eyes.** Make eye contact with the passer before the catch. Don't allow your defender to disrupt you, and don't worry about what Mom and Dad are hollering from the bleachers. You and your teammate must be on the same page. Eye contact tells the passer that you are ready.

▶ **Show hand targets.** Make sure your palm is facing the passer, almost like a catcher's mitt facing the pitcher in baseball. This gets your shooting arm in the L-shaped position, keeping you in shot line and increasing the likelihood that you will make the shot. Make a few shots and you'll receive more passes.

As a coach, you must stress to players that communication is an essential component of success. Calling for the ball reinforces this principle, but they still may be unwilling to take such initiative. If this happens, you may have to force your players to communicate. How do you do this? It's simple: Tell them that if they don't call for the ball, teammates won't pass them the ball. No exceptions. Your players must learn to demand the basketball and be confident that when they receive the pass they can make the shot.

Note that many coaches teach players to make a jump stop when receiving the basketball. In the case of shooting a straight-on, midrange jump shot, I very much prefer receiving with a one-two step. A jump stop is exactly as it sounds: you jump to the ball with both feet hitting the floor simultaneously, finding yourself stopped. Although you might be balanced and in an athletic stance, the problem with this method of receiving is that when you jump-stop, all of your power has stopped as well, and now you need to reload to get your shot off. Also when you stop, the defender becomes the aggressor because he or she can close out more easily and contest your shot. When you use a one-two step into the shot, you are the aggressor and have the defender backing up on his or her heels.

Release

With the ball called for and caught, you now need to explore the finer points of elevating and releasing the ball out of your straight-on, one-two-step shot. As the shooting foot comes forward, you push up, lift the body and straighten it out (see figure 5.3). The shooting foot should remain in a straight line to the target. The jump carries you up and slightly toward the target. This is due to the momentum of stepping straight on. The body should not turn or twist in the jump because this will pull the shot line off from the start. The arms lift the ball as the body moves upward. Hand positioning and grip will be unaffected because you caught the ball in the shot pocket. The shooting arm should remain in the proper L-shaped alignment before extending. Release the ball right before the top of the jump. If you wait until the top of the jump, your momentum will be on a downward swing, most likely causing the shot to fall short of the basket.

FIGURE 5.3 **Releasing the ball on a jump shot.**

Follow-Through

After you release the ball, you must keep your eyes on your target and freeze the follow-through. The shooting hand should be in a straight line to the target (hand in the hoop), and the elbow should be fully extended, finishing above the eyebrow and in front of the face, not behind the face or next to the ear (see figure 5.4). If the shooting hand finishes back by the ear, the ball will have too much arc. If you finish with the elbow below your eyebrow, you will be a streaky shooter who shoots line drives, and your shots will have a tendency to clang off the front or back of the rim. If you happen to actually make the shot, your makes will rattle in. There won't be many swishes.

One example of a player who initially struggled with his follow-through upon coming into the NBA is the Oklahoma City Thunder's Kevin Durant. If you watch him shoot, sometimes you will notice that his shooting elbow finishes below his eyebrow, and the arc on his shot is flat. He has made an effort in his short career to improve his shooting as evidenced by increasing his percentages. He is always working on his technique and shooting mechanics. Kevin is never satisfied with his shot and just recently won his third NBA scoring title. The great ones are always improving.

Now, with your follow-through extended and your elbow finishing above the eyebrow, you should consider what to do with your balance hand. The balance hand should remain on its own side of the body with the fingertips pointing toward the sky or ceiling at about a 45-degree angle. There should be no twist or turn with it. Do not drop the balance hand because this causes you to miss short and also pulls your shot line off as a result of negative motion. Your shooting hand extends *up*, and your balance hand remains still on the finish.

Always *shoot and stay* when shooting a jump shot from 15 feet (4.5 m) and farther. Many coaches make the mistake of harping on players to follow their shot. You hear it at every level. Understand that the longer the shot, the longer the rebound is off the rim if the shot is missed. This happens because players shoot jump shots with more strength than they do their shots in close. Begin practicing the shoot-and-stay concept with your midrange game.

FIGURE 5.4 **Following through on a jump shot.**

Pull-Up Jump Shot

The next step in the progression is to take what you've learned about shooting the straight-on, one-two-step midrange shot off the catch and applying those concepts to when you have a live dribble going. This skill is known as shooting a pull-up jump shot. When shooting the pull-up jump shot from straight on, you will need to use your dribble as a pass to yourself. To be successful, you must understand some key aspects of the dribble. First, you never want to dribble the ball outside of your body; instead, dribble out in front so that it leads you into the shot, just like a good pass would lead you into the shot. Second, you should be skilled at putting the ball down with either hand and being able to go either way with either foot as a pivot.

For the pull-up jump shot, you push the ball out in front and take a long stride with your *live* foot (see figure 5.5). By live foot, I mean the nonpivot foot. This will enable you to step into your shot with the same one-two step used previously. Also, the long stride of the live foot allows you to get low and to get past the defender. You should remember, though, that you must not dribble the ball straight down or you will inevitably dribble off your foot. Push the ball out and past the defender.

If you are a right-handed shooter and you are going right, you should pick up the ball with two hands into your shot pocket and then continue right into your shooting motion. If you are a right-handed shooter and you are going left, you will

FIGURE 5.5   **Shooter stepping into the pull-up jump shot.**

find that if you try to pick up the ball with two hands, you will be off balance. This is because you are reaching across your body with your shooting arm and pulling your *shot line* out of alignment. Instead, dribble the ball and allow it to come up into your left hand and then bring the ball across to your shooting hand. This is called *loading the gun,* because you load your shooting hand with your ammunition, the ball. Picking up the ball in this method is the most important part of the shot when going to your weak hand because it allows you to maintain alignment. When bringing the ball to the shooting hand, you must keep the shooting elbow tucked and in a straight line, your *shot line,* with the target. You will find that by doing this, your momentum moves forward and not backward or to the side, which is exactly the balance you are looking for when shooting a pull-up jump shot.

To practice the pull-up jump shot, begin with these two drills:

▶ **One-dribble pull-up drill.** Start out with the right foot as the pivot foot, and take a dribble going right before pulling up to shoot. You then return to the beginning spot and take a hard dribble going left, still using the right foot as the pivot foot and pulling up into the jump shot. Do this 20 times, giving you 10 repetitions in each direction, and then repeat the drill using the left foot as your pivot foot.

▶ **Two-dribble pull-up drill.** The concept and repetitions are the same as in the one-dribble drill, but now you use two dribbles to get a better and closer shot at the basket. Once again, work on going both ways with different pivot feet.

Shooting the pull-up jump shot is an introduction to shooting off the dribble. We will cover shooting off the dribble in depth in chapter 8.

Drills for Midrange Jump Shots

You can use countless drills to learn the midrange jump shot. These are just a few of my favorites. Although they are simple, they are effective. Keep in mind the fundamental technique of the one-two step that we have covered in this chapter. All of the drills are designed to help you become efficient using this method. It doesn't matter if you're practicing alone, with a partner or with an entire team, you should never lose sight of learning the actual skill. Remember, the skill makes the drill.

A final note on drilling the midrange jump shot: you can add faking elements. For example, say on Monday you practice a one-two-step, straight-on midrange shot in your spinouts drill. On Tuesday, perform the same drill, but add a shot fake. On Wednesday, add a jab step. On Thursday, jab, then shot-fake, then shoot. The proper technique for executing jabs and shot fakes is covered in chapter 8. The point is that when you are drilling, whether by yourself or with a partner, it should never become a boring process because there are so many skills to hone. In the basic midrange shot, you have the opportunity to master variations of the same weapon that will leave defenders frustrated and opposing coaches scratching their heads over how they might shut you down.

Spinouts

This is a drill that you can use when alone to simulate a catch-and-shoot opportunity. Start in a balanced athletic stance and spin the ball toward yourself so that it bounces off the ground and into your shot pocket. Time the spin and take a one-two step into the jump shot. You should freeze your follow-through until the ball hits the floor, allowing yourself to reinforce and ingrain this habit. Many players have a tendency to drop the balance hand or both hands on the follow-through. If you drop the hands quickly in practice, you will drop them more quickly in the game.

Make sure your spinout never comes above your waist. Start low and stay low until you pull up into your shot. By spinning out low, you will eliminate the high-low-high shot, in which you catch the ball and bring it down first, resulting in a negative motion and allowing a defender to get a hand on the ball, as well as taking more time to get the shot off.

Perform this drill 10 times from a single spot. Record the number of makes and shoot from seven spots, circling around the basket during any given routine. Once you've become comfortable with your midrange technique, progress from shooting 10 to actually making 10. If making

10 is a struggle, begin by making 5 and work your way up. The point I want to drive home here is that when great shooters practice, they go for *makes* and not *takes*. Another way to practice is to shoot *strings style* from the seven spots and see how many you can make in a row from each spot. Mix it up and keep it competitive for yourself. Be creative.

Partner Shooting

In this drill, players are paired up. You can perform this drill in a two-person workout or use multiple baskets for an entire team of players. One player acts as the shooter and starts in a balanced athletic stance. The shooter calls for the ball and the other player passes the ball from under the basket. The shooter takes a one-two step to meet the ball, catches it, sights the target, and shoots the ball. The shooter should strive to catch the ball in a balanced position and to land after the shot in a balanced position while freezing the follow-through. The shooter shoots from seven spots around the basket. The shooter can shoot in the same manner as he or she would in spinouts, either going for a certain number of makes or shooting strings style. Players can alternate shots and follow up their misses with a weak-handed layup. The important things to emphasize are that the shooter should use correct fundamental technique and the passer should deliver good passes. If you never practice throwing good passes in practice, you will never be able to throw good passes in games.

Closeout Shooting

This drill is like partner shooting, except that now, the passer will *close out* on the shooter after he or she passes the ball. A proper closeout is executed by sprinting directly at the shooter before taking several short, choppy steps to establish good defensive positioning and mirroring the ball with your hand to contest the shot. Adding closeouts from the passer will stop you from catching high and then going low for a high-low-high shot. As mentioned previously, going high, low, then high allows the defender more time to get to you to contest the shot or even stop you from shooting. You always want to go from low to high so you can shoot the ball efficiently and effectively. As you did in shooting with a partner, shoot closeout style from seven spots around the basket. Also, you can advance from spot to spot by shooting for a certain number of makes or shooting strings style, or shooters and passers can alternate shots and positions.

Triangle Passing

Divide players into groups of at least seven. The group includes one rebounder, three or more passers (all with balls), and three or more shooters. As shown in figure 5.6, players line up in a triangle formation with the rebounder (shown as R in the diagram) under the hoop, the passers (shown as P in the diagram) on an elbow, and the shooters (shown as S in the diagram) along the baseline. The first passer in line delivers a pass to the shooter's shot pocket. The first shooter in line is in a shot-ready position and calls for the ball, takes a one-two step to the ball and shoots the jump shot, freezing the follow-through. The rebounder gets the ball out of the net. Regardless of whether it's a make or a miss, the rebounder tries not to let the ball hit the floor. After getting the ball, the rebounder speed dribbles out to the passing line with the weak hand. The passer moves to the end of the shooting line, and the shooter becomes the next rebounder.

This is a continuous drill that allows a group of people to perform a lot of repetitions in a short amount of time. You can also change the pass from baseline to elbow and reverse the line rotation to practice shooting from another spot. Be sure to drill triangle passing on both sides of the court. I especially like this drill because the passing angle is more gamelike. In spinouts or partner shooting, the pass comes from under the basket, which is ideal for working on a one-two-step, straight-on shot. However, in a game, passes more often come from an angle. This drill allows players to simulate those types of passes while working on the same one-two step mechanics. You can keep the drill competitive by

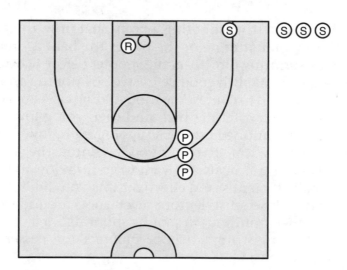

FIGURE 5.6   **Triangle passing.**

going for a certain number of team makes or having players track their own personal makes and having the losers run sprints. Many coaches like to put two minutes on the clock and run this drill from four spots—both corners and both elbows.

Transition Jump Shot

This drill teaches players how to make the transition from a sprint to being on balance for the jump shot. Divide players into groups of at least seven. The group includes one rebounder, three or more passers, all with balls, and three or more shooters. Shooters start at midcourt at either sideline and inbounds, and passers line up in the corner on the same side of the court as the shooters. To begin, the first shooter in line takes long strides and then shorter steps before timing the one-two step into the jump shot. It is important that the shooter calls for the ball, especially now that he or she is moving at a high rate of speed. When the shooter calls for the ball, the passer delivers the ball and tries to hit the shooter as he or she strides into the one-two step. The shooter receives the ball and takes the shot. The rebounder tries not to let the ball hit the floor, and after getting the ball, he or she dribbles to the corner where the passers are positioned. The first shooter now becomes the rebounder and the passer takes a position at the end of the shooting line. When practicing this drill with a group of players, make it competitive by going for total makes, or have the players compete against one another based on individual makes. You can also time this drill.

Stop and Pop

This drill helps players improve their pull-up jump shot off the dribble. It can be done individually or with an entire team. Players begin at either half-court or full court and use a speed dribble up the court. The player stops on a dime to shoot a 12- to 15-foot (3.6-4.5 m) jump shot. Perform this 10 times with each hand. When going full court, the shooter goes down to one end using the right hand and comes back using the left. More advanced players can work on using different types of dribble moves, incorporating a crossover dribble or an inside-out dribble before stopping and popping.

The next chapter looks at extending your range to behind the three-point arc. Understanding how to shoot the three and the value of the long-range shot itself is essential to becoming a complete player, but too many players all too often fall in love with shooting from deep and neglect to develop their midrange skills. Don't let that happen to you. As you continue with this book, you will see that we are building up to becoming not just a great shooter, but a great scorer as well. There has never been a truly great scorer in the history of game that didn't possess the ability to consistently hit shots from the midrange area. Perfect the midrange weapon. It's the cornerstone to evolving from a shooter into a scorer.

chapter 6

Long-Range Jump Shots

A long-range jump shot, or three-point shot, has become a vital part of today's game. Almost everyone thinks that he or she can make the three. Some coaches fully embrace shooting behind the arc and will live and die by that shot. Usually they are dying by it. It is difficult to shoot the three ball for an entire season and rely solely on it. Kids love it from the first time they step on the floor. After all, not everyone can dunk, but everyone can and will shoot the three, from small guys to 7-footers (2.1 m).

Before you can shoot the three, you must be able to make the two-point shot. We established that in chapter 5. Too many parents, coaches, and players are worried about the three-point shot. It seems that the younger and the smaller the kids are, the farther out they want to shoot from. Learn to make a stationary shot before extending your range. Another problem kids run into with long-range shooting is that the three-point line in high school and college is too close to the basket, making players believe that they can shoot from there when in reality they shouldn't. Players need to know what their shot is and shoot that shot. Too many players believe that they are three-point shooters when they can't even make a wide-open 15-footer (4.5 m).

That said, the three-point shot has become a larger part of every-one's offense, and we would be remiss to ignore its impact on the game. Coaches figure that if you shoot 33 percent from the three, that is the equivalent of shooting 50 percent from two-point range. Kids also shoot more threes simply because they are worth more. The problem is that too many young kids start out shooting threes and only threes. We should count ourselves lucky that there isn't a four-point line because if there were, kids would be shooting from even farther out. If you ever see young kids on an NBA floor, they will try to shoot from the deep NBA line simply because it is there. They shoot it because it is where the professionals shoot from, and who doesn't want to be like the pros?

For many of these young players, it takes every ounce of strength to shoot a three. When these kids are shooting threes, they are learning poor shooting form and technique. Some recreation programs don't allow the three-point shot. This is good for the younger kids because it forces them to shoot the ball within their range because there is no reward for a longer shot. They find themselves learning correct shooting form and technique. Depending on what level of basketball you play, the three-point line varies in distance. The high school line is 19 feet 9 inches (6.1 m). The college line is now 20 feet 9 inches (6.3 m). In international play, the three is 22 feet 2 inches (6.8 m). Finally, the NBA three-point line is 22 feet (6.7 m) away along the sidelines and 23 feet 9 inches (7.2 m) away spanning from one wing across the top and to the other wing.

Parents, players, and coaches always ask when kids should start shooting the three ball. It all depends on the player. Some kids mature physically at an earlier age and have the strength to shoot it sooner than others. If a kid's form is different from the three-point line than it is from inside the arc, it is probably not a good idea to begin shooting the three at this time. When the player gets older and stronger, then he or she will be able to shoot the ball with the same form.

Technique for Long-Range Jump Shots

To become a real threat from long range, you must be adept at catching and shooting the ball using different styles of footwork. There are two core styles to master: regular, straight-on, one-two-step technique and then progress to an on-the-move technique in which you pivot on your inside foot toward the target.

Shooting the Long-Range Jump Shot: Straight On

In the straight-on, long-range jump shot, you use a traditional one-two step, first with the nonshooting foot and then with the shooting foot, before catching and rising into the shot. Many three-point opportunities occur as a result of a pass thrown from the inside out. Therefore, it is essential to hone this skill.

First, let's clarify that the principles of shooting the long-range jump shot do not differ from the midrange shot discussed in chapter 3. For this shot, too, make sure that your stance is staggered with your feet shoulder-width apart, that you grip the ball properly, and that you shoot from the shot pocket. Make sure that your follow-through finishes with the elbow above the eyebrow and that you focus on connecting with the center of the basket. These principles never change. That's the beauty of shooting. The major variable that you have to concern yourself with on the long-range shot is the physical distance between you and the basket.

Because of the distance of the three-point shot, most players have to step into the shot to gain power and momentum. You should always be prepared before receiving the ball: the mind, feet, body, and hands should all be ready. You should also space out, or begin 3 to 5 feet (1-1.5 m) behind the three-point line, so that you can time your one-two step into the shot and generate the power necessary to shoot from that distance.

By taking a one-two step into the shot, you are getting your legs into the shot. This is essential when shooting from downtown. Your biggest and strongest muscles are in your legs, so use them. The one-two step should be slightly more pronounced to account for the longer distance. When taking a one-two step into a straight-on, three-point shot, right-handed players should step left to right and left-handed players should step right to left (see figure 6.1 for an example of a right-handed player stepping left to right). By doing this, you always bring the shooting foot into the shot, adding the momentum and power necessary to score the ball from this range. If you step with the shooting foot first, you are no longer stepping into the shot, and you won't generate power or momentum.

If you are a right-handed shooter, the ball should arrive in your shot pocket as your left foot is hitting the floor. Remember to step from heel to toe. When you step heel to toe, you transfer your weight forward into the shot. The younger you are, the more important it is to step into the shot to harness all of your strength and power to shoot the ball. Make sure to take a long stride when meeting the ball. The longer the stride you take when meeting the ball, the more power you will generate. Be aggressive when meeting the ball. By taking a long stride, you will remain low and eliminate any dip and negative motion in your shot, thus speeding up the shot. Remember, you always want to shoot the ball from low to high. The shot that goes high, low, and then high, or

FIGURE 6.1 **A right-handed shooter receiving the ball with a one-two step for the straight-on three.**

makes a dipping motion, slows your shot process and allows a defender to contest the shot.

As you lift the ball from your shot pocket and get into your follow-through, make sure to keep your elbow under the ball. Remember, you want to be a *lifter*, not a *slinger* or a *pusher*. Oftentimes, players compensate for the added distance of the three-point shot by altering the bend of their shooting elbow. No matter the distance of the shot, you should always maintain consistency in how you release the ball. When you shoot the three ball, make sure that you think *swish* and *shoot and stay*. Remember, the longer the shot, the longer the rebound. So when you shoot and stay, you have the opportunity to track a long rebound or to be an outlet pass for a teammate if he or she beats you to the ball. If the defense gets the rebound, you are in a good position to get back in transition. You should shoot, stay, then react.

Freeze your follow-through until the ball passes through the net. When you freeze your follow-through, you are more likely to shoot and stay. If you drop your follow-through, you are likely to have dancing feet. As a coach and an instructor, when I see shooters dropping their follow-through, it tells me that they weren't entirely focused on swishing the shot in the first place. If your hands are moving, there is a good chance your feet are moving. This signifies that you were not balanced. You should never attempt a long-range shot if you are unable to receive the ball in a balanced shot-ready position.

Once you have mastered the straight-on, catch-and-shoot three, you should develop the shot off the dribble, known as the pull-up three-point shot. Whether you are dribbling with your left or right hand, your one-two step will remain the same: left to right if you're right handed and right to left if you're left handed. The major difference will be in how you pick up the ball. If you are dribbling with your strong hand, you will pick up the ball into your shot pocket with two hands (see figure 6.2). Note, however, that when you are dribbling with your weak hand you need to bring the ball across your body and *load the gun* (see figure 6.3).

Shooting the three off the dribble is something that you should practice, but it is not the type of shot that you are likely to shoot in high volume in a game situation. This shot is typically seen at the end of a fast break, where the offense has a numbers advantage but not necessarily an advantage inside for a high-percentage layup. The ball handler may then elect to shoot the straight-on, pull-up three off the dribble. Even still, your coach may advise you not to settle for that shot and to attempt to force the issue at the rim. Make sure that you and your coach communicate and not only understand the difference between a good shot and a bad shot, but also are on the same wavelength regarding the shots your team wants.

FIGURE 6.2 Picking up the ball to shoot a three when dribbling with the strong hand.

FIGURE 6.3 Picking up the ball to shoot a three when dribbling with the weak hand.

Shooting the Long-Range Jump Shot: On the Move

Shooting the long-range jump shot on the move refers to a player moving from left to right or right to left before squaring up to the basket to shoot. Shooting on the move in screening situations will be covered in more detail in chapter 9, but it's important to begin discussing the basic techniques here because long-range three-point shots are often available through on-the-move situations. Many coaches design cross-screen situations for good shooters in which the shooter moves toward the ball while outside of the three-point arc before catching and facing the basket and then rising into his or her shooting motion.

Once you've mastered the straight-on, catch-and-shoot three and the three off the dribble, you should develop your ability to shoot the three on the move. Practice on-the-move shooting both as a catch-and-shoot shot and as a shot off the dribble. When first starting, for a right-handed player, spin the ball out to yourself or have a teammate pass to you while you are moving from left to right, staying outside the three-point arc and moving toward the passer. Move right to left if you are a left-handed player. Start in an athletic stance, feet shoulder-width apart, knees bent, shoulders and head down, your hands ready, and the shot pocket formed. Come to the ball and meet it. When you are ready to catch the ball, take a long aggressive step toward the ball with the left foot, but open the step up toward the target (see figure 6.4*a*). The heel-to-toe step is vital now because you must be able to pivot into your shot, squaring up to the basket. If you step flat footed, your shot will be slow, and you may fail to square yourself to the target.

Once you make the catch, you must bring your shooting foot, the right foot in this case, into the shot (see figure 6.4, *b* and *c*). The right foot should be in a straight line facing the center of the basket. You do not want to overstride. If this happens, you will not create a good shooting foundation and will find yourself off-balance. Also, if you overstride, you will be out of alignment with your shot line, leaving yourself susceptible to missing left or right.

When the shooting foot hits the floor, explode into your jump for the three-point shot (see figure 6.4*d*). Just like in a straight-on shot, begin to straighten your body to be able to shoot the ball. The shoulders and head rise upright so you can see the target. Release the ball right before the top of the jump. By releasing the ball right before the top of the jump, you will maximize your power. This is an essential concept for shooting the three-point shot. The momentum of the shot will force you slightly toward the target. You should not drift in the direction you are moving. By getting low before the catch, you position yourself with a lower center of gravity and will shoot better because you will be balanced from the time you receive the ball and up until the shot is finished.

FIGURE 6.4   A right-handed shooter receiving the ball for the on-the-move three.

Moving from right to left for a right-handed shooter requires slightly different technique. The player must continue to be low and balanced, but this time the right-handed shooter will step into the shot with the right foot. There will be no power or momentum from the right side of the body when getting into this shot. The approach will be the same: athletic stance, head and shoulders down, hands ready, and stepping to meet the ball. When the shooter is ready to receive the ball, he or she will step into it with a long aggressive step with the right foot (see figure 6.5*a*). It will once again be a heel-to-toe step. The shooter should open up toward the target with the right foot and right shoulder. The right foot has now become the pivot foot. It should point toward the target. Now the player must *stub* the left foot so that the base of the shot is the same as it is for every other shot (see figure 6.5*b*). This stub technique is the key difference in mastering a three-point shot on the move when moving from right to left for a right-handed player and left to right for a left-handed player.

FIGURE 6.5 A right-handed shooter stubbing the toe when moving from right to left for the three.

Once both feet are planted and the shooter is squared up, he or she must continue moving from low to high and jump into the shot (see figure 6.5c). Note that if the player fails to stub the toe and brings the left foot too far forward, the left side of the body will be the lead side, and the shooter will be forced to turn or twist the body during the shot. When this happens, the shot line will be off, causing the shot to miss either to the left or right.

The next step in your long-range shooting progression is mastering the three-point shot on the move from off the dribble. If you have trouble shooting off the dribble from straight on, you will have even more difficulty shooting off the dribble when moving from side to side. Once you are comfortable with the straight-on shot and have the footwork down, you can begin developing the shot on the move with your live dribble. Shooting on the move with a live dribble uses the same footwork as when shooting on the move off a pass. When moving from left to right if you are a right-handed shooter, you will dribble with your outside hand, which would be the right hand, and plant the inside foot, which would be the left foot (see figures 6.6, *a* and *b*). When getting ready to shoot, you must open up the left side of the body using a heel-to-toe step with the left foot. This heel-to-toe step enables the left foot to point toward the target as you square to the basket. You must also open up with the left hip and shoulder. Opening up in this fashion provides you with good peripheral vision, allowing you to see the entire court and anticipate whether or not the shot is about to be challenged by a nearby defender.

FIGURE 6.6 **A right-handed shooter pivoting into the three while dribbling on the move.**

Now that you have planted the left foot, bring the right foot around into the shot (see figure 6.6c). The ball should be coming up off the floor and into the shot pocket as the right foot comes around. Make sure to stay low. The toes of the right foot should point toward the center of the basket. The hip, shoulder, ball, and elbow should all be aligned with the center of the basket as well. Note that a left-handed shooter will follow the same steps just described, except that when picking the ball up, he or she brings the ball to the left hand and *loads the gun*. Also, a left-handed shooter *stubs* the right foot in order to maintain a common base with the left foot in front. In shooting the three-pointer when moving from right to left, the right-handed player would load the gun and stub the foot in the same fashion as the left-handed shooter did when moving from left to right. Always use your last dribble as a hard dribble. This

Long-Range Jump Shot: Game Situations

Most coaches like to get the ball inside first before kicking it out for the three-point shot. This is called inside-out basketball. Other coaches like to skip pass across the court for the three, or kick it ahead in transition for the early long ball. Some players like to pull up off the dribble at the three-point line in transition. When hugging the three-point line, you must also learn to shuffle-step, either right or left, into the three (see figure 6.7, *a-c* for an example of a shuffle step to the

FIGURE 6.7 **Shooter taking shuffle steps to the right when hugging the three-point line.**

(continued)

right). A shuffle step is the same movement as a defensive slide. It's a difficult technique to master because you are not moving toward the basket. The easiest threes occur when you are stepping into them because all of your momentum is going into the shot. These types of threes derive from a skip pass, inside-out situation or a drive-and-kick situation.

The most difficult threes derive from when you have to shoot going away from the basket or are shooting the three off the dribble with a shuffle step. This is because you no longer have forward momentum. Even though I don't recommend taking shots such as these in high volume, you still must practice them. If your league uses a shot clock, you will not have the luxury of patiently working toward the perfect one-two-step, three-point shot. Instead, you must practice and prepare to shoot a variety of three-point shots.

While developing the long-range shot from straight on, off the dribble, and on the move, you can also add faking elements to shuffle-step threes. Practice a shot fake before shooting your three, or jab at the basket before regaining your balance for the shot. Fake a shot, shuffle-step left with a dribble, and then pull up to shoot. Make the same move with a shuffle-step dribble to the right. Although the combinations are endless, you should drill yourself on these various shots so that when the clock winds down, you will be ready.

will give you more height on your jump and a quicker shot. The harder the bounce, the quicker and higher your shot will be—a must when shooting the three ball.

Drills for Long-Range Jump Shots

There are no hidden secrets to drilling the long-range three ball. It is simply an extension of the drills covered so far. The only difference is that now, you're going to extend your range behind the three-point arc. Great players keep building their skill set until they are virtually unstoppable. However, keep in mind that you should have a solid midrange game in place before you begin practicing drills from a distance.

A good way to begin drilling long-range jump shots is by using one-handed and two-handed form shooting. You should start close, practicing your alignment with and without your balance hand and making five shots before backing up half a step until you are shooting from long range. Once finished, begin a series of spinouts if you were working alone, or go into partner shooting if you are with a teammate. Shoot straight-on, catch-and-shoot threes from seven spots around the arc. You can shoot for a specific number of makes from each spot and chart the results, or you can shoot *strings* to see how many shots in a row you can make before moving on to another spot. Another way to approach shooting drills is to use the *three strikes* method. This means that you give yourself three misses before moving on to the next spot.

I can't stress enough how important it is to record the number of shots you make from each shooting spot, no matter what style you choose to practice on any given day. Recording your shots provides you with valuable information regarding where you shoot well from and where you need improvement. The more you understand about your own talent, the more effective you will be in a game. You can take these drills and mix up the style of long-range shots. Maybe one day you work on the straight-on, catch-and-shoot three, and the next day you work on the pull-up three off the dribble.

Once you've mastered the skills in the drills for one- and two-handed shooting form, begin incorporating the long-range three on the move. As we discussed briefly with midrange shooting, you can add faking elements to your long-range shooting. You can add a shot fake or a jab step to simulate freezing a defender or creating space before elevating into your shooting motion. The fundamental technique for executing various fakes will be covered in detail in chapter 8.

Shooting the three is probably the second most tempting style of shot next to attempting the highlight-reel dunk. And remember, not everyone is able to dunk, but everyone is able shoot the three. However, just because you are *able* to hoist the long ball does not mean that you are *capable* of making the shot consistently. But this doesn't mean you should neglect developing your shot from long range. The important thing to keep in mind is that you don't want to become a one-dimensional player. If all you do is practice the three, then all you will be able to do is shoot the three. If a defender gets all over you, what are you going to do? Don't become infatuated with the three-point shot and make it the focal point of your game. Instead, approach it as you would any other shooting or scoring skill: it's just another weapon to add to your arsenal.

chapter 7

Bank Shots

Shooting the ball off the backboard, or the glass, is known as the bank shot. It's funny how few players today use the backboard when shooting, but instead slap it with authority when attempting a layup because they think it looks cool. So, why don't more players use the backboard? Because those shots do not make the highlight reels. The bank shot is a very high-percentage shot. It is often taught to beginners, but then somewhere along the way coaches stop teaching it and players stop using it.

Years ago, many players used the glass when shooting: Sam Jones, Elgin Baylor, Jo Jo White, Elvin Hayes, George Gervin, Rudy Tomjanovich, Larry Bird, Magic Johnson, Julius Erving, Bill Bradley, Scottie Pippen, Bill Walton. The list of pre-1990s NBA players is extensive. In today's game, only a handful of players use the glass. The best bank shooter in the NBA today is Tim Duncan, or as Shaq calls him, the Big Fundamental. What Duncan lacks in NBA-level athleticism, he makes up for in sound fundamentals. The bank shot has been a major key to his offensive success. Dwyane Wade and Kobe Bryant also use the glass on occasion. Even so, not enough players use the bank shot anymore, making it a dying shot, along with the hook shot.

If you want to see great bank shots at the college level, do yourself a favor and look up footage of the legendary John Wooden's UCLA teams from the 1960s and '70s. They used the backboard with great success. Not only did John Wooden and UCLA win more championships than any other team in the history of the NCAA, but Wooden is also considered to be the greatest college basketball coach of all time. Every player on Wooden's teams could shoot the bank shot because it was a large part of practice every day. Wooden drilled a two-on-zero break with the ball handler in the middle of the court and the other player running the floor wide and then angling in for a layup. He would then change the shot to a stop-and-pop jumper off the glass and eventually extend the distance of the shot to a more traditional pull-up bank shot.

My goal for you is that by the end of this chapter, not only will you have an understanding of how to shoot the high-percentage bank shot, but also you will feel compelled to make it a part of your shooting practice. Let's make the bank shot cool again. I like to think of it like fashion, where trends come and go, but everything eventually repeats itself. I don't see any reason why the bank shot can't be brought back in style.

Bank Shot Technique

In terms of technique, the bank shot is similar to the jump shot; however, there are a few differences, such as the target and the angle at which it is shot. Otherwise, the stance, the arm position, and how you receiving the ball, release it, and follow through are all the same. Let's take a look at these in more detail.

Target, Angle, and Distance

For a bank shot, instead of targeting the middle of the basket as you do for a jump shot, you target the top of the small square painted on the backboard. Aim for the corner that is closest to you (see figure 7.1). If you hit this target, the ball kisses off the backboard and drops through the net. It's that simple. Without taking into consideration proper shot mechanics or release and follow-through, it's curious that the bank shot isn't more widely practiced given the fact that the target is so easy to locate. Of course, making the shot is more difficult if there is no square on the backboard, but I haven't come across a hoop in modern basketball that doesn't have that little box painted neatly on the glass. You should focus on this target, and just like in the traditional jump shot, you should never take your eyes off the target. Keeping your eyes on

FIGURE 7.1   On bank shots, aim for the corner of the square. Target the corner that is closest to you.

the ball throughout its flight is a mistake on any shot because you fail to focus on where you intend to place the ball.

An issue many players have when considering whether to use the backboard is when and where to use it. What is a good banking angle? Where on the court is too far out to use the glass? Some players think that when they shoot a bank shot, they must shoot higher and harder. This is a common misconception. With practice, you will eventually develop the touch for shooting off the glass. The shot mechanics will be the same no matter the distance from the hoop. The key in knowing when to and when not to bank the shot is being aware of your angle on the floor in relation to the basket.

The rule for bank shots is that whenever you are at a 45-degree angle to the basket, you should use the glass out to 15 feet (4.5 m). A good mark on the court to use to determine whether you are at a 45-degree angle is the low-post block. Your ideal angle is just above the block and extended out to 15 feet (4.5 m), or where the foul line might be if it were positioned along the sides (see figure 7.2). When you flatten out toward the baseline at an angle below the low-post block, shooting a bank shot becomes more difficult, and you should avoid it. Anything farther out than 15 feet (4.5 m) requires exceptional skill and touch. Tim Duncan is that rare exception. He has phenomenal touch and can bank from farther out and from more difficult angles than others. But the reason he can do this is that he has worked to make this an integral part of his game. It's possible to master the art of the bank shot, but it takes many hours of practice. Focus on perfecting the shot at a 45-degree angle and out to 15 feet (4.5 m) before experimenting with other angles and distances.

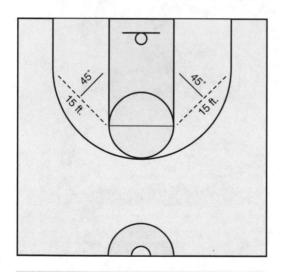

FIGURE 7.2 **Angles and distances of bank shots.**

Often, when players get into a position where they have a good angle for a bank shot, they second-guess themselves and wonder whether they should or should not bank it. This habit of hesitating almost always results in a miss because the shot comes up short and the ball doesn't get high enough on the glass. First of all, shoot the ball. Don't hesitate. If you don't take the shot, the result is always the same: a miss that didn't have a chance. To become more

Shooting a Bank Shot Off the Dribble

When shooting a bank shot off the dribble, you must remember to go somewhere with that dribble and then pick up the ball correctly. Recall from chapter 5 that when going to your strong hand, you want to pick up the ball with two hands, right into your shot pocket. When you are going to your weak hand, you *load the gun* and bring the ball into your shot pocket.

Practice from behind the three-point line and combine fundamental skills. For example, work on a shot-fake-and-go move (covered in detail in chapter 8) and finish with your bank shot. This allows you to economize your practice time. It's important to not only work this shot from both sides of the court, but also to execute the move going both to your left and right on either side of the hoop. You never know how a defender is going to close out on you, so you have to be fully prepared to attack your defender in either direction. For example, sometimes a defender is in a bad position as a result of a good screen and is forced to close out on you favoring your left even if he or she wanted to make you go left. Other bad defenders just can't remember which way the scouting report told them to close out. Then there are other really bad defenders who don't know whether you are right handed or left handed. Regardless, it's important for you to practice the move going in either direction from both sides of the court so that you are ready to exploit these defenders no matter the situation.

When you shot-fake, stay in your athletic stance and keep your feet still as you raise the ball to your head. Once the defender has left his or her feet, it is time to go past. Put the dribble out in front of you and either use the one-two step or the jump stop. Yes, I said jump stop. When using the jump stop, make sure to land on two feet, shoulder-width apart and with the shooting foot slightly in front and the knees bent (see figure 7.3, *a* and *b*). Note that you're still landing in an athletic stance. Using the jump stop in this scenario prevents you from overpenetrating and picking up an offensive foul. Jump stops are an effective technique to use when attacking a crowded paint area. Oftentimes, players shoot the pull-up bank shot because they are unable to get all the way to the rim. Therefore, it is important that they are in full control. This is only one of two times that I advocate practicing with a jump stop. The other is in a scenario where you are catching the ball with your back to the basket, in which case you are not in position to act as the aggressor offensively.

(continued)

Shooting a Bank Shot Off the Dribble (continued)

FIGURE 7.3   Making a jump stop before rising into a bank shot.

confident using the bank shot, visualize the ball hitting the top of the square, banking off the board, and then swishing through the net. As you learned in chapter 2, visualization is a large part of successful shooting. To develop confidence in this shot, you must implement drills into your practice that use the bank shot. If you emphasize that the shot itself is important and make it a part of your daily training, then you will eventually be able to shoot it with confidence.

Bank Shot Drills

With an understanding of your new offensive weapon in place, it's now time to practice the bank shot. Following are drills that you can and should implement into individual and team practices. Recall that John Wooden made the bank shot a large part of practice every day. And who was he? Oh, yeah, just some legendary coach whose teams won more championships than any other in the history of the NCAA. Believe me, the bank shot had its place in a handful of those championship rings.

Bank Shot Form Shooting

This uses the same setup as the drills for one-handed and two-handed shooting form covered in chapter 3. The only difference is that now you will shoot from the 45-degree bank-shot angle along both sides of the basket. You start at midcourt, tight to the sideline, and dribble down the sideline until you are at a 45-degree angle for the bank shot. Make five shots, then move out half a step at a time until you are 15 feet (4.5 m) from the basket or until your form breaks down. Once you've performed the drill in the one-handed style, repeat the series two handed. It's the ideal warm-up shooting drill before you begin practicing the bank shot at game speed.

Close-to-Midrange Spinouts

The next progression after form in bank shots is to perform the bank shot in your familiar one-two-step, catch-and-shoot motion. You want to work both sides of basket, shooting the shot from in close and then working your way out to 15 feet (4.5 m). As in your other shooting routines, you can work toward making 10 shots from each spot, or you can shoot strings style.

Under-the-Basket Spinouts

The bank shot, or more specifically, the turnaround bank shot, is an offensive weapon that is especially useful when scoring in the low- to mid-post area and shooting over a smaller defender. It's a skill that takes many hours to perfect because you must become competent catching and squaring off either pivot foot and making the shot from both sides of the court. However, if you can perfect the technique and become comfortable shooting the turnaround bank shot off either pivot foot, you will discover that the shot itself is virtually unguardable. Let's look at how a right-handed player would shoot the turnaround bank shot on the right side off either pivot foot.

Begin on the low block and perform a spinout toward the wing area at a 45-degree angle. Take a few short, choppy steps before taking a longer stride with your left foot. This will be your pivot foot. For this series, make an inside pivot in which your shooting foot, your right foot, opens up toward the middle of the floor to a point where you are in *shot line* and ready to elevate and shoot the bank shot. Make sure that you catch the ball low off your spinout so that when you square to shoot the bank shot, you will be doing so from low to high.

Now, from under the basket, spinout and jump stop to catch the ball. Your back will be to the basket. Practice all four of the pivots: outside right, outside left, inside right, and inside left.

Strive to make 10 of any variation of the shot that you choose to practice. In this example of the right-handed shooter shooting on the right side of the basket, make 10 using your left foot as a pivot foot and making an inside pivot, and then progress to pivoting on your left foot and making a front pivot where you turn toward the baseline. Once you've made 10 of those, make 10 more using your right foot as your pivot foot off an inside pivot, and finish with 10 makes pivoting on your right foot using a front pivot. That's 40 makes from one side of the floor. Make sure to practice the same variations from the other side as well. You may not want to tackle every variation in one workout, but you should be aware that there are four basic ways to pivot and square when shooting the turnaround bank shot, and then strive to master each method.

Pull-Up Bank Shot

The last method for perfecting the bank shot is by drilling the shot as a pull-up shot off the dribble. We've already talked about practicing the move off a shot fake, but you could also incorporate a jab step or even begin outside the three-point arc along the wing area with a live dribble. Like with all your shooting workouts, mix it up and keep it fun and engaging. You want to attack until you are 12 to 15 feet (3.6-4.5 m) away from the basket. Recall from chapter 5 that when you practice shooting pull-up jump shots, you want to use the dribble as a pass to yourself. Therefore, it is essential that you dribble the ball not outside of the plane of your body, but rather out in front so that you can use your normal one-two step into the shot as if you were receiving a pass.

You also want to make sure to practice dribbling into your pull-up bank shot with either hand and from both sides of the court. If you are a right-handed shooter, start at midcourt, tight to the sideline. Dribble down the sideline until you are at a 45-degree angle for the bank shot and speed dribble toward the lane. Attack until you are five to ten feet from the basket. Then pull up for the bank shot. The goal is to make 10. Once you've finished that, attack by dribbling the ball with your left hand, and then *load the gun* to maintain alignment before pulling up into your bank shot. Make 10 of this variation and then repeat the series on the other sideline.

Work to make the bank shot a part of your game. As I stated at the beginning of this chapter, this is not a skill that is likely to wow the crowd or get you onto the next highlight reel, but it's a fundamental skill that can vastly expand your scoring opportunities. If you can become efficient at banking shots from the midrange area, you will discover that you have the ability to attack taller, longer defenders with confidence. By banking the ball off the glass, you will shoot the ball at a higher trajectory, enabling yourself to put the ball up and over a player who is looking for that blocked shot worthy of a highlight reel. Instead of making the defender the unsung hero of the top 10 plays of the day, make him look foolish by nailing a bank shot right in his face.

chapter 8

Creating
Your Own Shot

Once you have become competent shooting the basketball from a stationary position, and you are capable of knocking down a jump shot off a one-two step, and you have learned to shoot on the move with either pivot foot, you next must gain the ability to create your own shot when you find yourself contested. Some players may think that creating your own shot means that you put the ball through your legs three times and behind your back a half a dozen times before shooting. This is not what creating your own shot is about and is nothing but one-on-one selfish play. When you create a shot on your own, you must do so in the flow of the game and in the structure of an offense.

In today's NBA, no one is able to create his own shot quite like the Los Angeles Lakers' Kobe Bryant. However, that wasn't always the case with Kobe. When he first came into the league, Kobe was that one-on-one selfish player who tried to do it all himself. Then he became teammates with Shaquille O'Neal and discovered how to play off a great big man. The duo dominated the league, and Kobe began to come into his own. However, when O'Neal departed, Kobe fell back into a pattern of trying to continuously be *the man* night in and night out. While his individual scoring numbers were staggering, his Lakers team wasn't winning. Within the past three seasons, Kobe has matured into a finely tuned scoring machine, conscious of getting his teammates involved before creating his own offense as the game closes. As a result, the Lakers have once again reclaimed their throne as the NBA's most dominant franchise, and much of that is directly related to Kobe's improvement as a decision maker.

You should strive to be a more efficient player by using moves and fakes and spending less time dribbling the ball in place. Another great way to be a more efficient offensive player is to spend more time moving without the ball, setting screens and then coming off screens. The more you are able to come off screens and move without the ball, the less you will have to concern yourself with creating your own shot. We will discuss more about coming off screens and moving without the ball in chapter 9. This chapter is dedicated to the specific movements you will use to create a shot under defensive pressure with the clock winding down.

What are you going to do when you have three seconds or less on the short clock and no time to go into your dribbling routine? You better have practiced this situation at some point, and if you are a real player, then you should have prepared yourself for this moment and done it over and over again, thousands of times at your local gym or even in your own driveway. What real basketball player doesn't thrive on the idea of scoring that game-winning bucket? That's what we live for. Before you start getting into making your moves to create space, study some of the great NBA players and watch and take notes on how they get their shots off. Just think how great these players are and how defenses are geared toward shutting them down, and yet they are still able to get off good shots against a top-notch defender time and time again.

Current NBA players to watch once they catch the ball include Kobe, Carmelo Anthony, LeBron James, Dwyane Wade, Dirk Nowitzki, Paul Pierce, Tim Duncan, and Chris Bosh. All of these players have the ability to create their own shots. Some of these players are very athletic, and then there are others who are just proficient at executing fundamental skills. These players use their smarts to get their shots off. Also if you can, watch tapes or go on YouTube to find clips of Michael Jordan, Larry Bird, Hakeem Olajuwon, Reggie Miller, Chris Mullin, and Steve Smith. These are just a handful of historically great players who had great moves and could always create their own shots.

The reason most players don't work on creating their own shot and being able to shoot off the dribble from a variety of catching situations is because it is extremely hard work. There are several players on every level who are great shooters if they are allowed to stand still and if they have time to get their shot off. If you allow them these luxuries, they will be sure to shoot a high percentage. But if you put them in a game situation against a top-notch defender who closes out quickly, their game will go to complete shambles because they have never really practiced shooting off the dribble or worked on creating space and have certainly never done it quickly.

You have an understanding of how to practice to become a great shooter. Now it's time to take it to the next level. You want to become a great scorer. To be a truly great scorer, you must be able to do it all. You must be able to make shots while stationary, you must be able to catch and shoot, shoot it off the dribble, create off the dribble, and also create using jabs and fakes.

Going by the Defender

Before we get into using fakes and jabs to get a defender off balance, you need to have a basic understanding of how to go by your defender off either pivot while protecting the ball. When you go by a defender, you are either going all the way to the rim or getting into your pull-up jump shot as first detailed in chapter 5. Let's be clear that a pull-up jump shot is a shot off the dribble and that the major difference between shooting off the dribble and shooting off the catch is that you are in control of where you go. In this case, you want to go by your defender, so it's essential that you push the ball out in front of yourself and cover some distance with this dribble. Pushing the ball out allows you time to get your legs under yourself and properly use a one-two step into your pull-up jump shot. This is about dribbling with a purpose.

When you are creating your own shot and going by a defender, you are moving north to south instead of east to west. Think about it in this scenario: you catch the ball at the three-point line and your defender is tight on you. When you dribble by, you want to be tight to the defender and push the ball forward, turning a contested three-point shot into an open 15-footer (4.5 m). While dribbling, you want to be under control and make sure that your hand closest to the basket or defender is used to protect the ball. We call this the *arm bar* because bars are used to protect us and keep people out, in our case, a pesky defender (see figure 8.1).

When you have your arm bar up, it should be bent in an L-shape with your hand in a fist. By closing your hand in a fist, you tense those muscles, making the arm bar stronger. If your hand is open, the defender can easily knock down the arm bar, and if there is no foul called, the defender is likely to get a hand on the dribble and come up with a steal. Note that when you form your arm bar, you must keep it tight to your body. Extending it out and away will cause you to initiate contact with the defender you just went by and get called for an offensive foul. Also, keeping the arm bar tight allows you to maintain good balance and keep yourself in proper positioning to rise into your pull-up jump shot.

If you are a right-handed shooter going to the right past your defender, you will use your left arm as your arm bar. When you pull up into your jump shot, make sure to open the fist of your arm bar and pick up the ball with two hands upon establishing your shot line and getting into your shot (see figure 8.2, *a-c*). If you are right handed, but driving left, you would use your right arm as your arm bar. This requires you to open your fist and *load the gun* upon establishing your shot line and getting into your shot (see figure 8.3, *a-c*). For a left-handed shooter, it's the opposite; *load the gun* when going right and pick up the ball with two hands when going left. Now that you understand how to go by a defender while protecting the ball, you are ready to explore how to get that defender out of position in the first place and create your lane to the basket.

FIGURE 8.1   **Using an arm bar to protect the ball.**

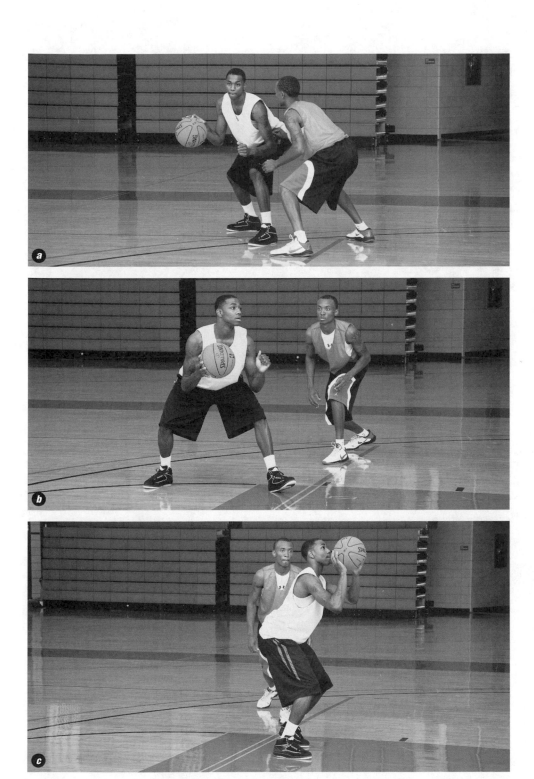

FIGURE 8.2 A right-handed shooter using an arm bar when going to the right past a defender.

FIGURE 8.3   A right-handed shooter using an arm bar when going left past a defender.

Fakes

Fakes are maneuvers an offensive player uses to move a defensive player out of position. Once the defender is out of position, the offensive player is able to create a scoring opportunity. We are going to cover two key fakes in great detail: the shot fake and the jab step. When learning to shoot off fakes, always think shot first. This way, you will always be low, in a shooting position, on balance, and ready to play basketball. You always want to maintain the triple-threat position in which you're prepared to shoot, pass, or drive the ball. Many players use fakes, but oftentimes they will overextend on a jab step or straighten up on a shot fake. These mistakes make it impossible for them to react quickly and give the defender time to regain positioning. Staying low and athletic, along with having solid footwork are the keys to maintaining good balance and executing good fakes whether they be shot fakes or jabs.

Shot Fakes

Just like it sounds, a shot fake means faking a shot. The shot fake is a valuable weapon to add to your arsenal because every defender wants to block a shot. It doesn't matter how short or tall he or she might be, all defenders have an inner desire to leap up in the air and attempt to bat your shot away to the cheap seats. Coaches can work on closeouts all they want, but the tendency in game situations is for players to run out at a shooter completely out of control and find themselves flying through the air. The shot fake capitalizes on this natural instinct of the defender. You want to block my shot? Well here's your chance. With a properly executed shot fake, the offensive player will take the defender out of the play and find himself with an easy scoring opportunity.

To execute a shot fake, start in a balanced, athletic stance with the knees bent. You should be facing the basket with your eyes on the target. Lift the ball to your head while keeping your knees bent (see figure 8.4). This position will allow you the option to either shoot the ball immediately if your defender doesn't react or to go to the hoop by putting the ball on the floor and stepping into your pull-up jump shot (a *show-and-go* move, which will be discussed in the next section).

Make sure that when you lift and show the ball on your shot fake, you keep your feet still. Many players take a negative step, as shown in figure 8.5, when attempting a shot fake, meaning that when they lift the ball, their foot steps away from the basket. Concentrate on keeping your feet still and avoid taking a negative step so you are able to go right into your shot or to the hoop for your pull-up. Many referees will call you for a traveling violation on a negative step simply because it doesn't look right. Also, if you take a negative step while positioned in the corner, you're likely to step out of bounds because of the limited space.

Finally, your shot fake should be executed at the same rate of speed as your normal shot. Too many players fake too fast. Allow time for your defender to react and then make the correct scoring decision.

FIGURE 8.4   **A shot fake.**

FIGURE 8.5   **Incorrectly stepping back when using a shot fake.**

Remember, a fake is not a fake if it looks like a fake. Think about the last sentence and study it. When you make a shot fake, you want it to look like a shot not a shot fake. Most players' shot fakes during games look unnatural and cumbersome because players only practice these moves when coaches tell them to execute shot fakes in a certain practice drill. Think about the amount of time coaches actually spend on shooting each day in practice. If coaches spend 30 minutes each day practicing shooting, which is on the high end, how much time can they spend on shooting where you have to create your own shot, use shot fakes, shoot off the dribble, come off screens, and so on? There simply isn't enough time for coaches to teach shooting the correct way in a variety of scoring methods. So, as a player, you must put the extra time in and continue working on your game. How good or how great do you want to be?

Once you've become comfortable practicing the shot fake from a stationary position, it is time to work on this move in your spinout routine or work on the move pass-and-catch style with a teammate coming from straight on. Practicing with spinouts or pass-and-catches allows you to drill yourself under more gamelike conditions. I like to develop this skill first from the top of the key area and then progress to shooting from seven spots. Because you will be drilling at game speed, you can begin adding more movement into your fakes.

Remember to keep your feet still, stay in your athletic stance with your knees bent, and bring the ball up to your head on the shot fake. After using the fake, shoot the ball and freeze your follow-through, keeping in mind the same shooting mechanics you've been learning throughout this book. Staying low on the shot fake is essential. If you straighten up, you will have to bend at the knees and the waist to regain a sense of balance before rising and shooting. When you lift the ball up to fake, make sure you stay in your *shot line*. You will lift the ball and bring it back to the shot pocket, and then you will go immediately into your shot. You can drill the shot fake, by going for a certain number of makes from various spots, shooting strings style, or even shooting three-strikes style. Once you're comfortable with the shot from midrange, practice it from long range. Remember, you are working on this move in a straight-on catching situation. That means you will always begin by receiving the ball using your normal one-two-step catching technique before getting into your scoring move.

And, finally, once you've worked on making a shot fake then shooting from a straight-on catch, work on it on the move going left to right and right to left off your inside pivot foot. I like to work this move from either wing, spinning out toward the baseline and then out toward the middle of the floor. For example, if you are a right-handed shooter practicing the shot fake then shooting from the right wing, you would begin by making 10 shots spinning out toward the baseline and pivoting off the left foot. Once finished, you would spin toward the middle, pivot off the right foot, and make 10 more. You would then repeat the routine from the other side of the court, keeping in mind the principles of receiving on the move. That's a total of 40 makes.

Of course, you can also practice shooting strings style or three-strikes style. Once comfortable from midrange, work on the shot from long range. As always, when you pivot on the move, make sure you are balanced and properly aligned to the basket. If you are practicing pass-and-catch style with a teammate, you can close out on each other and alternate shots while keeping an individual score. Once a player reaches a certain number of baskets, he or she can be declared the winner and the loser has to run a sprint.

Show-and-Go

The show-and-go is a move in which you shot-fake and then go somewhere with the dribble. Depending on how the defender closes out, you must be able to show and go both right and left. You cannot predetermine the direction that you go in. For example, if you anticipate going right and the defender close out on your right side, you would likely pick up an offensive foul. When you show, see where the defender is and go in the appropriate direction. There are only two options: a strong-side show-and-go and a weak-side show-and-go.

In a strong-side show-and-go, the player will put the ball on the floor with the strong hand and drive by the defender in that direction. A weak-side show-and-go is just the opposite. To become a great scorer, you must be able to go both ways. It's essential that you not only develop your scoring moves, but that you also learn how to read the defense. As you develop your show-and-go, you will become more precise in terms of your decision making as a scorer.

When performing the show-and-go to either the strong or weak side, you must stay in your shooting stance with the knees bent so that you can explode by the defender without having to reload the body. If you were to come out of your stance and lock your knees, you would allow the defender time to regain position and take away the drive. Also, remember your arm bar. That defender you just faked out of his shorts is likely to try to scramble back in front of you and poke at the ball. You must always remember to protect the ball as you go by, no matter what fake you're using. In terms of the skill progression of the move, develop the show-and-go to the strong and weak sides first off a straight-on, one-two step, and then progress to catching on the move and using the inside pivot foot.

Strong-Side Show-and-Go

In a strong-side show-and-go, you will go by the defender off a dribble using your strong hand. In a straight-on catch, if you are a right-handed shooter, you will receive the ball with the normal one-two step. This means that the shooting foot, right foot, would be your live foot (see figure 8.6*a*). Your pivot foot would be the left foot. Show the ball and then step with the right foot past the defender, as shown in figure 8.6*b*, with the dribble out in front of you, not to the side. Always go by a defender, not around a defender. After the dribble, jump-stop into your jump shot (see figure 8.6*c*). Although I have previously mentioned that I don't advocate the jump stop, this is an especially great time to use it. When using a show-and-go move, it's likely that you will be attacking a set defense. This means once you get by your defender, help will be ready. The jump stop prevents you from overpenetrating and picking up an offensive foul. Of course, if the help is not set, then you would take the ball all the way to the basket.

FIGURE 8.6   A strong-side show-and-go off a left then right step into the shot.

After mastering this, a right-handed player would then progress to executing a strong-side show-and-go after making an on-the-move catch. The footwork for the show-and-go is identical to the straight-on situation if you are moving from left to right and pivoting on your nonshooting foot. In this case, it is the left foot. However, when moving from right to left, you will be pivoting inside on your shooting foot. As you catch the ball in this fashion, make sure to stub your toe as you square to the basket. Because you are still working on a strong-side show-and-go, you must shot-fake (see figure 8.7a) and then use a crossover step with your left foot to seal the defender off (see figure 8.7b). Always put the dribble out in front of you, and once again, come to a jump stop before shooting the jump shot (see figure 8.7c). You must be able to show and go right no matter what pivot foot you use.

FIGURE 8.7   **A strong-side show-and-go off a right then left step into the shot.**

Weak-Side Show-and-Go

A weak-side show-and-go is a move in which you go by the defender off a dribble using your weak hand. To execute a weak-side show-and-go, raise the ball to your head on the shot fake and then rip the ball down and over to your opposite hip. If you bring the ball down on the same side after the shot fake, the defense has a chance to make a play on the ball or knock the ball free. It will also take you more time to get the ball across your body. Use a weak-side show-and-go when the defense closes out on your shooting hand.

You develop the weak-side show-and-go in much the same manner as you do the strong-side show-and-go. First, practice the move in a straight-on catch situation where you are taking a one-two step to the ball. Make sure to stay low and on balance on the catch. One difference when executing the weak-side show-and-go in a straight-on situation is that you will shot-fake and go using a crossover step to seal the defender. For example, if you are a right-handed player, during your straight-on, one-two step, your left foot is the pivot foot. After the shot fake (see figure 8.8 *a* and *b*), your live foot, or shooting foot, steps across your body when you dribble the ball with your left hand (see figure 8.8*c*). After making this crossover step, jump-stop the same as you would using the strong-side show-and-go and pull up into your jump shot (see figure 8.8*d*). Note that on all weak-side drives, you will have to *load the gun* in order to shoot the ball on balance and in proper alignment.

Once you become proficient at the move from a straight-on catch, progress to catching on the move. If you are a right-handed player, the footwork of the weak-side show-and-go remains the same when moving from left to right on the catch. This is because you are pivoting off your left foot, requiring you to do a crossover step with your right foot and drive left after you've shot-faked. Once you advance to moving from right to left, work on stubbing your toe on the catch, show the ball, rip it to your hip, and dribble by with your left foot (see figure 8.9, *a-c*). This produces an open step rather a crossover step.

Like everything you've learned thus far, you have to develop the show-and-go move in stages. Whether you're drilling a spinout or with a partner, begin working on both the strong-side and a weak-side show-and-go from a straight-on catch from the seven shooting spots. Go for makes or shoot strings style or three-strikes style. To develop the strong-side and weak-side show-and-go on the move, work the shot from the wing areas. Spin the ball out toward the baseline from one side and then out toward the middle. After that, work the other side.

Once you've become proficient at both the strong-side and weak-side show-and-go moves, you can work on learning how to read your defender. The show-and-go move is perfect in a closeout drill situation. Have a teammate throw you a pass and close out either to the left or to

FIGURE 8.8   **A weak-side show-and-go from a straight-on catch.**

the right. You must make the correct read: if they defender closes out left, show and go right and vice versa.

Once you've become comfortable making reads, you can turn the drill into a live, competitive one-on-one game. If the offensive player scores, he or she gets to stay on offense. If the defensive player gets a stop, he or she gets to go on offense. To work on this with the whole team, break the team into groups of three or four at a basket and turn it into a one-on-one-on-one competition. If the offensive player scores, you get a new defender. Each player keeps track of the number of baskets he or she scores. After five minutes of drilling, the player with the most points is declared the winner. Competitive drills such as one-on-one-on-one out of a closeout situation are a great way to develop a scoring mindset.

FIGURE 8.9 A weak-side show-and-go while moving from right to left.

Jab Step

The jab step is a short, quick movement at the defender with the non-pivot foot. The primary purpose of the jab step is to get the defender off balance in order to gain an advantage so you can attack. If you jab at the defender and he or she gets back on his or her heels or retreats then you can go right up into your shot (see figure 8.10). Make sure that you always jab short and jab at the defender. If you jab to the side or jab too long, you will no longer be in your stance and your balance will be off. A defender may react to this kind of jab step, and you may think you have gained an advantage, but because it was to the side or too long, you will have to regather yourself, allowing the defender time to get back into a defensive position.

When executing the jab step, be efficient in your movement. The jab only needs to be 1 or 2 inches (5 cm) forward. From that position you should still be able to rise up and shoot a jump shot on balance, or pull back and jab again, or jab and go to the basket. If you jab at the defender a few times, it stands to reason that you will eventually get him off balance and create a scoring opportunity. However, it is essential to be aware of what your teammates are doing as you jab. If you take too long to make your move, not only may you miss a teammate for a better scoring opportunity, but you also allow the help defense to get set and

FIGURE 8.10 A jab step.

stop any move that you make once you get past your own defender. Always make concise and precise moves. Finally, when learning the jab step, make sure you can jab well with your shooting foot before advancing to the jab step with your nonshooting foot.

Because we always begin practicing our moves in a straight-on catch situation, it stands to reason that your shooting foot, right foot if you're right handed and left foot if you're left handed, will always be your nonpivot foot, or jab foot. However, when you catch on the move, you pivot on your inside foot. This means that your jab step might come from your nonshooting foot. You have to work up to this skill. One of the best players ever at jabbing with either foot was Andrew Toney of the Philadelphia 76ers. Andrew was a right-handed shooter, but whenever he found himself with his right foot as his pivot foot, he would simply jab at the defender with his left foot. The defender would retreat and play Andrew for the drive. After all, how could anyone shoot with the left foot slightly in front of the right foot if he was a right-handed shooter? Well, Andrew could, and he would go right into his jump shot and knock it down.

I remember seeing Andrew Toney kill the Celtics with the left-footed jab step. I went to the courts and started working on it immediately. At first it seemed a little bit awkward. After all, it takes the lower body out of proper shot alignment. But after doing it over and over, it became more comfortable, and I too was knocking shots down. I was able to prove to myself that no matter what the skill, if I worked at something hard enough, I could perfect it and add it to my arsenal. It was a valuable lesson that I picked up late in my career while I was playing professional basketball in Ireland. You are never too old to learn new tricks—the question is how great do you want to be? There is always something in your game that you need to work on. Don't just work on things to work on them, work on them to perfect them.

Begin practicing your jab step from a stationary position. Jab with your shooting foot and then rise up into your shot. Once you are comfortable with the move, work on it as a straight-on move, receiving the ball from a spinout if practicing alone or pass-and-catch style with a teammate. Make sure when catching straight on that you use your normal one-two step, pause, and then jab into the jump shot. Otherwise you are likely to one-two-step directly into your shot and convince yourself that it was a jab step. The pause also allows you the opportunity to read the defender. In this case, the defender retreats, so you rise and shoot. Shoot this shot from your seven spots going for makes, shooting strings, or shooting three-strikes style. Once you've mastered it from the midrange area, extend it out to the three-point line. Every great three-point shooter in the history of the game has relied heavily on a jab-rise-and-shoot move. Take it from Larry Bird, Reggie Miller, and Ray Allen, no serious three-point threat is complete without honing this skill.

Progress to working on the jab step on the move and perfect the skill by using both pivot feet. Drill the jab-step move from either wing, spinning out toward the baseline and then toward the middle. Note that when you find yourself pivoting on your shooting foot and jabbing with your nonshooting foot, you will be working on that Andrew Toney–style shot mentioned previously. This might feel a little awkward at first, but it's essential to develop if you intend to master the jab-step series.

Finally, you can also work on a jab-and-go move into a pull-up jump shot. Remember, the jab is a short, quick step. The idea is to threaten the drive, causing the defender to back off and enabling you to rise and shoot. A good defender will eventually recognize this fake and stay up on you to contest the shot. Because you have jabbed short and are still low and athletic, your body is coiled and prepared to drive by the defender and get into your pull-up in much the same manner as in a show-and-go move. You should work a strong-side jab-and-go as well as a weak-side jab-and-go. Begin drilling jab-and-go moves in the same fashion: first off your straight-on, one-two-step catch from the seven spots and then on the move, pivoting on your inside foot and spinning out toward the baseline and the middle from either wing.

With the complete jab skill set in place, you should now compete against a teammate and learn to make the correct reads. Have a defender close out on you after passing so you can develop instincts that will serve you well in a game. Should you rise and shoot? Attack left into a pull-up? Or attack right into a pull-up? You can keep score against one another and play to a certain number of points and even deduct points for making incorrect reads, e.g., a defender closes right and the shooter attempts to jab and go right, likely resulting in a player-control foul. It's important to remember to progress the skill at a comfortable pace. Become adept at simply jabbing and shooting from a straight-on pass before attempting to jab and dribble into a pull-up, pivoting on your shooting foot while on the move.

Step Back

The shot-fake and jab-step moves are executed while keeping the goal of attacking the defender in mind. Let's say you beat your defender with a shot fake or jab and get yourself into the lane with the dribble. You look for your pull-up jump shot, but a second help defender contests you. To create space, you use a step-back maneuver in which you step back and away from the help defender to create a new scoring opportunity. This is one of the most advanced techniques for a great scorer to master.

The step back is an effective move for getting your shot off the dribble by using your inside pivot foot to push off and create the space necessary to shoot comfortably and on balance. Note that a correctly executed step-back move always begins with a push off using the inside pivot foot. If you use your outside foot to step back, you create very little space. You are pulling your body back with your outside foot instead of pushing off with your inside foot. It's a slower movement that a defender can easily stay with.

There are two types of step-back moves to consider: the weak-side step back and the strong-side step back. The weak-side step back is learned first because it is easier to grasp and easier to execute than the strong-side step back. This is because the strong foot, or shooting foot, is planted, resulting in less motion than the strong-side step back and allowing you to maintain your shot line in relation to the basket.

Weak-Side Step Back

The weak-side step back is called so because the shooter will step back at an angle to his or her weak side. So, right-handed players will step back left and left-handed players will step back right. To perform the weak-side step back, drive hard and low at the defender, plant the inside foot between the defender's two feet, and push back off it, hopping back or stepping back with the back foot to create space. This move is easier when you are dribbling to your weak side because you will plant your shooting, or strong-side, foot.

For example, assume you are a right-handed shooter going from right to left. Plant the right foot, which is the strong-side foot, (see figure 8.11a) and push off that foot to create separation for the shot (see figure 8.11b). Pushing off the inside, or strong-side, foot allows you to create

FIGURE 8.11   **A weak-side step back.**

more space when pushing back and allows you to maintain balance because you are stepping backward with no drift in the step back. No drift means that you will be able to perform a weak-side step back without drifting or squaring to the target because you are already in shot line. In the next segment, you will see that this is the major difference between executing a weak-side step back and a strong-side step back.

Once you have stepped back and created space, land on balance in a shooter's stance with the shooting foot slightly in front of the other foot. The toe should be pointing toward the target, the knees should be bent, the shoulders should be in front of the feet, and the head should be in front of the shoulders. If the shoulders are not in front of the feet when you land, then when you bring the ball up into shooting position, your weight and balance will go backward, which will cause the shot to fall short.

Strong-Side Step Back

Once you've become comfortable with the weak-side step back, begin developing the strong-side step back. In a strong-side step back, you dribble with your shooting hand, going to your strong side. You will step back at an angle to the strong side. To execute a strong-side step back, plant your inside, or nonshooting, foot (see figure 8.12*a*) and hop or step back to create space (see figure 8.12*b*). You now must drift or square yourself toward the direction you are going so you are able to maintain

FIGURE 8.12 A strong-side step back.

your shot line in relation to the basket. You land on balance in your shooter's stance and have now created enough space to rise and shoot. The movement of the strong-side step back for a right-handed shooter looks more like a checkmark than when executing a weak-side step back, as shown in figure 8.13. It is important to stay low when performing this move. If you are too upright, you will find yourself drifting in the direction of your dribble and will shoot the ball fading away and off balance.

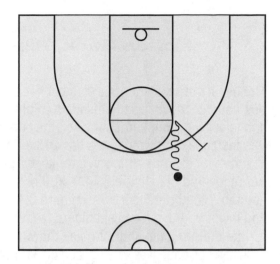

FIGURE 8.13 **Path for a strong-side step back.**

Before you begin drilling any of the scoring variations of the step-back maneuver, make sure you have the footwork down. This move needs to be built from the ground up. Whether you are working alone in a spinout routine or with a partner, begin drilling yourself from the top of the key area. Start first with a weak-side step back: attack the paint with your weak hand and plant your shooting foot. Step back at an angle, staying in shot line and landing on balance. Go for a certain number of makes or shoot strings or three-strikes style. When starting out, you should attack the paint deep enough that when you use the step back, you will be shooting a midrange shot.

Once you become comfortable from midrange, you can use a step-back maneuver from farther out so that you will be shooting a long-range three. After you've drilled the weak-side step back, follow the same routine drilling the strong-side step back. Remember, with a strong-side move, you will attack the paint with your strong hand and plant your nonshooting foot. As you step back, you will have to square yourself to the target to achieve proper alignment as you rise for the shot.

Once you've completed drilling your shot with a step-back move from the top of the key and using a live dribble, progress to working the same shot with an on-the-move catch. Get into your now familiar on-the-move routine in which you work from either wing, spinning out toward the baseline and then spinning out toward the middle. Note that you will need to work on driving with both the weak hand and strong hand when spinning out from any given angle. To clarify, that's four ways to get into your shot using a step back from either wing: driving weak and strong when spinning out to the baseline, and driving weak and strong

Step Back, Rise Up, and Go

The beauty of mastering the step back is that it lends itself to an equally dangerous counter move. Good defenders might be able to close the space you create and take away your shot, but when they do, they open up a lane to the basket. In this instance, you would step back, rise up, and go. To execute this move, let's assume, for example, that you have used a step back and the defender has reacted but recovered (see figure 8.14*a*). You raise your head and shoulders up like you are about to shoot the ball (see figure 8.14*b*). As the defender is coming at you, you lower your head and shoulders, and blow by the defender (see figure 8.14*c*) for the pull-up jump shot or go all the way to the rim for a layup.

When you step back, rise up, and go, you can explode by either dribbling with the same hand, or if the defender closes out on the dribble hand, you can incorporate a crossover dribble. To clarify, let's look at a right-handed player who executes a weak-side step back, as shown in figure 8.15*a*. With this particular move, the player will dribble with the left hand before pushing off the shooting foot to step back at an angle. As the shooter steps back, the ball will still be dribbled with the left hand, but as the defender closes to that side, the shooter can immediately cross over and dribble by going right before getting into the pull-up jump shot (see figure 8.15, *b* and *c*).

Develop the step back and go and step back and cross over using the same method as you would for the step-back shot. First, work each move from the top of the key off a live dribble. Execute the step back and go and step back and cross over off both a weak-side and a strong-side step back. Once you've become comfortable off the dribble, get into the same on-the-move routine, spinning out toward the baseline and out toward the middle from either wing.

FIGURE 8.14 Step back, rise up, and go.

FIGURE 8.15 A crossover dribble in the step back, rise up, and go move after using a weak-side step back.

when spinning out to the middle. Make sure to work both sides of the floor. Once you've become comfortable shooting from midrange, you can begin developing the shot from long range.

Drilling in this fashion is also a great way to combine skills that you've already learned and incorporate them into this routine. For example, say you are a right-handed shooter working from the right wing and spinning out toward the middle. As you catch on the inside pivot foot, you will have to work on stubbing the toe as you initially square to the hoop. You can then work on a shot fake before ripping to the hip and driving baseline using a crossover step. With the ball in the strong hand, you will get into a strong-side step-back shot.

By incorporating multiple skills in your routines, you economize practice time, which can help speed your development as a player. However, it's important that you focus on fundamentals in the execution of each skill and don't become sloppy as you build from one skill to the next.

Combination Scoring Moves

By now, you should understand what it takes to be a scorer. We've covered shooting in great detail, but you should not limit yourself to being just a standstill shooter. You must create your own shots off the shot fake, jab step, and step back, and then be able to progress into a combination of moves in order to be able to go past the defender. Be a scorer. For example, you must be able to shot-fake and then go somewhere with the dribble if the defender doesn't bite on the initial shot fake. Or, if you jab at a defender who doesn't retreat on the jab, you must be able to jab and go by. We have already touched on how to string multiple moves together to get your shot off and also create space. Following are a few of my personal favorite combination scoring moves.

Jab and Shot Fake

As the name implies, in this move you combine the jab and shot fake and execute them at the same time. This move is similar to the show-and-go in that you might use it when a defender closes out on you. When you use this move, defenders are forced to defend against the drive as well as the shot. I have found this move to be most beneficial for midrange post players. In today's NBA, Kevin Garnett comes to mind. By jabbing and shot-faking at the same time, KG puts other big men in limbo. They don't want to fully commit to contesting the shot because they are threatened by the drive. What happens is that the defenders close out soft, meaning that they leave plenty of space between themselves and the player they are guarding. The shot fake also causes defenders to straighten up on their closeout, which makes it difficult for them to jump with any elevation and contest the shot. The end result for KG is plenty of time to knock down his patented midrange jumper.

To execute the jab and shot fake in combination, jab-step hard at the defender while raising the ball to the head just as you would on a normal shot fake (see figure 8.16). Some players even like to sell the move with a slight head fake as well. Head fake simply means that you tilt the head back as you raise the ball with the shot fake. It adds an element of salesmanship that is sure to freeze the defender and leave you wide open for the jumper.

FIGURE 8.16 **A jab and shot fake in combination.**

Jab, Jab, Jumper

Jab once. The defender stays. Jab again. The defender retreats. Open jump shot. The jab, jab, jumper, as shown in figure 8.17, *a-d*, is built on the premise that if the first jab does not work, then the second is sure to. Defenders get better and better at higher levels of play. As you develop and progress into an offensive scoring machine, you will find yourself guarded by the opposing team's number one, lockdown defender. He or she has been instructed not to bite on your first fake. So why not give the defender two? Even the all-time-great one-on-one defenders such as Joe Dumars, Dennis Rodman, Michael Cooper, and Bruce Bowen and in today's NBA, Ron Artest, bite on multiple fakes. The jab, jab, jumper is a great move to possess when you need to get your defender off balance. Remember not to overstride on the first jab. You won't be in a decent shooting position and you will not be in an athletic stance. Keep the jabs short and quick. Some players can jab three or four times quickly and still maintain a good, balanced shooting position. Work on the jab, jab, jumper, jabbing with both your shooting foot and nonshooting foot. Become adept at the skill and you will have no problem keeping your defender on his or her heels.

FIGURE 8.17 A jab, jab, jumper.

Jab, Jab, and Go

Jab once. The defender stays. Jab again. He still stays, but this time he is frozen. He remembers a few possessions ago where you got him on his heels and knocked down the shot. This time, he's not backing up. But he is paralyzed. Stuck in the mud. Frozen. So blow by him. It is essential that you do not limit yourself to being just a jump shooter. You must also be able to get to the basket. On the jab, jab, and go, as shown in figure 8.18, *a-c*, make sure that your last step is a long step past the defender. Attack right along the defender's hip and brush against him. Also, remember to use your arm bar to protect the ball and stay strong. When driving by a defender, it is important to stay really tight, because this will keep him off balance and actually open up his stance. It's almost as if he is like a bull fighter, taunting you with his cape and inviting you to go to the hole. So do it. Be a scorer. Push the ball out past where you step so that your dribble covers a lot of distance. Once you are by and the ball is protected, you must regain control and determine if you will pull up for a jump shot off the dribble or go all the way to the rim.

FIGURE 8.18 A jab, jab, and go.

Let's face it: the possibilities really are endless. You could catch, shot-fake, jab, shot-fake again, go into a weak-side step back, and then cross over and go into a pull-up jump shot. The thing about becoming a great one-on-one scorer is not to get too caught up in stringing moves together. If you find yourself thinking about this while playing, chances are you'll be executing the moves under slow conditions and against a set defense. The shot-fake, jab-step, and step-back moves are skills that need to be drilled until they feel like second nature. Don't try to learn all the moves at once. You will wind up being inefficient and mediocre at everything. Even the greatest scorers have an understanding of what moves are their very best. When the game is on the line, they'll go to that move, and if the defender takes away the initial look, the scorer is prepared because he or she has honed a counterattack to his or her favorite, patented game winner.

As a player, you must experiment to get a feel for what you like to do, but then narrow it down and perfect that skill in a variety of catching situations: first the straight-on, one-two step, then the on-the-move catch when pivoting on your nonshooting foot, and finally catching on the move when pivoting with your shooting foot. Once you've mastered your move from all of these positions, you can take on a new move and build your arsenal until you are truly unstoppable. Kobe Bryant of the LA Lakers is always working on new moves. He watches tapes, studies the defense, and then he goes to the gym and visualizes a defender playing him. His next step after doing the same move over and over is to grab a teammate to play live defense. Kobe will work on the same move against live defense until he has mastered it. Then he will use the move in a game. Chances are it works because of all of his preparation and repetition.

Shooting and Scoring Off Screens

Being able to catch and shoot on the move is an essential skill to perfect if you are to become effective as a player receiving a screen. In this chapter, we reinforce catching and shooting on the move and learn about how to apply it in various screening situations. As a skilled offensive player and scorer, you want to be prepared and give your teammates a reason to screen for you.

Technique for Coming Off Screens

When coming off screens, assume a balanced athletic stance with your knees bent. Also bend at the midsection and bring your head and shoulders down (see figure 9.1). You want to stay low until you get into your shooting motion. If you are low coming off the screen and are low catching the ball, you will be ready to play basketball and make a move if you are unable to take the initial shot. You don't want to come off a screen high and have to use more motion or time with a low-high movement that allows a defender time to recover and take away the scoring opportunity created by the screening action. Always keep in mind the low-to-high principle. It makes you quicker and more efficient as an offensive player.

FIGURE 9.1   **A low, balanced position when preparing to come off a screen.**

A lot of coaches teach kids to come off screens shoulder to shoulder, and that is where players get into the habit of falling off balance. This will cause you to be too high when coming off the screen, and when you have to turn and square up, you will have a high center of gravity that causes you to drift in the direction you are going. The correct way to come off a screen is body to body, with your shoulders meeting the waist or hips of the screener (see figure 9.2*a*). If you come off the screen this way, you will be low and balanced, prepared to shoot or make a move. If you come off shoulder to shoulder at game speed, you will consistently be off balance as a result of being too high (see figure 9.2*b*). Good balance will give you a good chance at making shots on the move. The more balanced you are, the better your chances will be of making the shots. Don't be lazy coming off screens. This is an opportunity to score. Come off screens hard and make hard cuts to free yourself from your defender.

FIGURE 9.2   *(a)* Coming off a screen in a body-to-body position; *(b)* coming off a screen in a shoulder-to-shoulder position, which is too high.

Before coming off a screen, you must set up your defender by getting into him or her with your body (see figure 9.3). This forces the defender to play tight to you, so when you push off with your feet and head toward the screen, your defender is likely to trail and get caught. Another option is to take the defender away from the screen first by making a V-cut toward the basket before popping out and rubbing the defender off the screener (see figure 9.4). You want to be in an athletic stance coming off the screen, staying tight and making contact with your screener. Remember, it is not a foul to hit your teammate. Do not leave space for the defender to get through or over the screen. If you do that, the screen is worthless. Make sure that your hands are ready and the shot pocket is formed as you come off the screen. If your hands are ready, they will be the first thing that the passer sees, and this gives him or her a good idea of where you want the basketball.

When you come off screens, you are catching on the move. Therefore, you want to plant your inside foot when receiving the basketball. This will give you a couple of advantages as an offensive player that you won't have if you come to a jump stop. First of all, you will have better body control and balance. Second, you can see the floor better if you use the inside pivot foot. By opening up your body toward the basket with your hip and shoulder as you plant the inside foot, you are able to see

FIGURE 9.3   Shooter receiving the screen, gets into the body of his defender and pushes off and has a step on the defender before he comes off the screen.

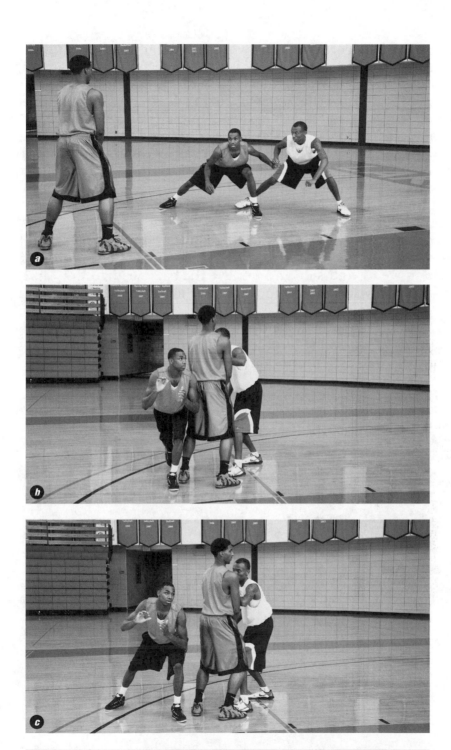

FIGURE 9.4 Shooter receiving the screen *(a)* takes the defender away from the screen, then *(b)* quickly changes direction using a V-cut and moves back toward the screener, *(c)* allowing a step on the defender as he comes off the screen.

where your defender is by using your peripheral vision (see figure 9.5). By seeing the defender, you can make a better decision upon catching the ball. For example, if the defender is close to you and has fought through the screen, you know that you will be unable to rise into an immediate jump shot and instead may have to get into one of your scoring moves. When you come to a jump stop instead of using the inside pivot, you lose sight of the defender because you will be jumping square to the teammate passing you the ball (see figure 9.6), then squaring up to the basket while in the air.

Another reason to catch off your inside foot while on the move is the possibility that the pass will be bad. If the pass is thrown behind or to the outside of you, you can still adjust and make the catch if you plant the inside foot. By planting the inside foot, you can push off that foot to move to your side and retrieve the ball (see figure 9.7*a*). If you jump-stop, your feet will be in the air as the ball is in the air (see figure 9.7*b*). Not only will you be unable to quickly change direction, but if you can't see your defender and he or she winds up deflecting that pass, it will almost surely lead to a turnover. Always remember that possession is more important than position.

FIGURE 9.5   **Shooter catching the ball while planting the inside foot when coming off a screen.**

FIGURE 9.6   Shooter using a jump stop, which causes the shooter to lose sight of the defender.

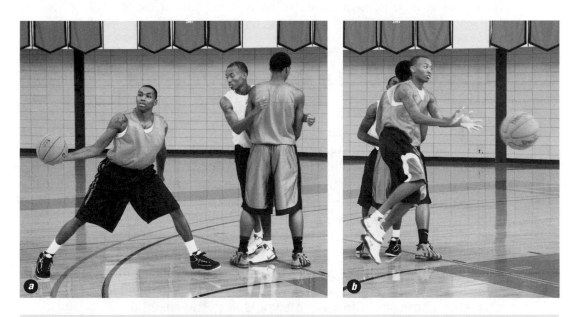

FIGURE 9.7   (a) The shooter can push off the inside foot to retrieve a bad pass after planting the inside foot, but if using a jump stop, (b) the shooter's feet are in the air when the ball is in the air.

Lastly, if you can see your defender and anticipate being open, you will get into your shot more quickly off an inside pivot than off a jump stop. The one-two step off your inside pivot allows you to step into your shot as the aggressor. With the jump stop, your momentum stops, and because you are moving sideways to the passer, it becomes even more difficult to land on balance and then square up to the target.

You must work on your footwork and timing when moving from left to right or right to left. The key is to make sure you stay low when coming off the screen. This will allow you to properly time your footwork. When stepping into the shot, you must learn to open up the inside pivot foot by planting the heel first. You want to transfer your energy and balance by catching while you land first on your heel and then shift your weight to your toe. If you do not plant your heel and instead land flat-footed, your shot will no longer be a one-two-step shot in rhythm, but more likely a three- or four-step shot in which you're forced to dribble to regain balance.

Another problem that occurs when you land flat-footed is that you are not positioning yourself to immediately square up for the catch-and-shoot opportunity. If you are moving toward the passer, it is impossible to plant flat-footed with your toe to the target. By stepping heel to toe, you will notice that your inside pivot foot naturally squares itself to the basket as you come around with the rest of your body. Stepping heel to toe ensures that you will always be balanced.

Drills for Coming Off Screens

The footwork for shooting on the move goes hand in hand, or rather foot in foot, with coming off screens. No matter the angle at which the screen is set and the angle at which you come off it, you will plant your inside foot before squaring and shooting. Therefore, you must be adept at shooting on the move. Practicing shooting on the move is something that most players don't do on their own. Players have a tendency to just practice spot shooting from different areas on the floor. Spot shooting is good, and it is necessary for perfecting your technique, but in a game, most of a player's shots are on the move. These are *game shots*. Don't just practice shooting stationary jump shots alone. You must practice shooting game shots from game spots at game speed.

Before you begin practicing shooting on the move at game speed, I strongly recommend that you practice spinouts, moving left to right and right to left, but without shooting the ball. If you do this, you can focus on your footwork. Start out at half speed. Once you are comfortable and are doing it correctly and have a good, balanced foundation, increase the speed of the spinouts. When you are able to square up at game speed without being off balance, you can add the shot.

You need to fully understand how to square yourself to the basket off either pivot foot while maintaining alignment to the target. You must have the footwork down before you can work on shooting at game speed. If you don't do something right the first time, when will you do it right? If you aren't doing something correctly in practice, you won't all of a sudden do it correctly in a game.

Make sure that you carry what you've learned from one drill over to the next. So many players have a tendency to forget about their follow-through and finishing their shooting motion because shooting on the move requires them to concentrate on their footwork. Just because footwork is the focus, do not lose sight of the end goal: swishing the shot with proper form.

Around-the-World Spinouts

Start out on the right baseline with your back to the wall at the three-point line. The entire court should be in front of you, and you should be in a triple-threat position. The starting point will be at the baseline at the three-point line. Begin the drill by spinning the ball toward yourself and out onto the court along the three-point line. The ball will bounce off the floor and back toward you, simulating a pass. You now must run into your shot by using the inside pivot foot; in this case it would be the left foot. Once you have caught the ball, square up and align yourself with the target. You must be balanced with correct foot positioning. You should make several spinouts going around the world, or around the three-point arc, before reaching the other side of the baseline.

Once you reach the opposite side of the baseline, come back to the starting position and repeat the drill, or you can start on this side, performing the drill in the opposite direction. You can perform this drill alone or in a group. You should remember to start low and stay low and make sure to plant the correct pivot foot and then square up with your body and align yourself to the basket, assuming correct foot positioning and balance.

Spinouts To and From the Baseline

In this drill, you are working on the same skills as when you performed the spinouts to the middle in the previous two drills. However, now you are spinning the ball in a different direction. You should practice catching and shooting off spinouts from a variety of passing angles. In this situation, if the ball comes to you from the top, you would receive a down screen. A down-screening situation is one of the most common at virtually any level of play. In it, a teammate has set a screen at an angle *down* toward the baseline, enabling you, the shooter, to free yourself moving toward the ball. If the ball comes to you from the baseline, you would receive a screen off an inbounds play, which is another common screening situation geared toward generating a quick catch-and-shoot opportunity. You still are planting your inside foot to the target when receiving the ball, just as you've been practicing. Also make sure to work on shooting the ball from both sides of the basket, spinning out to and from the baseline.

The teaching points that we are emphasizing are to plant the inside foot as usual and then stub your foot when appropriate to maintain a proper shot line when squaring to the basket. For example, if you are a right-handed shooter working on catching a pass off a simulated down screen on the left side of the basket, you must make sure to plant your left foot and then bring your right foot all the way into your shot. However, if you are a left-handed shooter practicing the same move from the same side of the court, you would plant your left foot and then stub your right foot to maintain proper shooting alignment.

Left-to-Right V-Cut

This is a great team drill. Use two baskets and split the team into groups of 8 and 7 if you carry 15 players. As shown in figure 9.8, position one player near the basket in a rebounding position (shown as R in the diagram). That player's job is to keep the ball from hitting the floor. That seems like a little detail, but actually, it's a big detail. Rebounding can be taught, and that aspect of the drill emphasizes the importance of rebounding. It's all about developing a "get after it" mentality, having the hands up, hustling, and running down the ball.

Three or four players, all with balls, form the passing line on the right side of the floor, free-shot line extended and outside of the three-point line (shown as P in the diagram). Their responsibility is to work on making good passes, hitting the shooter in rhythm and in his or her shot pocket. If players can't make good passes in practice, how are they going to make good passes in a game with defenders harassing them? The remaining players will form the shooting line on the left-hand side of the floor, free-shot line extended and outside of the three-point line, facing the passing line (shown as S in the diagram).

The drill begins with a shooter taking an imaginary defender down toward the basket for several steps and then making a V-cut by pushing off his or her inside foot, left in this case, and then coming to meet the ball, as shown in figure 9.8. Shooters will call for the ball to let the passer know that they are open, ready, and catch in rhythm. Shooters must form their shot pocket, plant their inside foot, catch on balance, shoot on balance, and land on balance. After shooting, the shooters stay and freeze their follow-through. This builds on the principle of shooting and staying when attempting a perimeter shot, thus allowing them to track a potential long rebound. The rebounder retrieves the ball and then speed dribbles to the end of the passing line, preferably with his or her weaker hand. The passer sprints to the end of the shooting line. The shooter now becomes the rebounder.

After mastering the left-to-right, V-cut drill, players can perform the right-to-left, V-cut drill, going from the other side of the court. The rotations are the same: the rebounder dribbles to the end of the passing line, the passer sprints to the end of the shooting line, and the shooter becomes the new rebounder. The only difference is that players now push off their right foot when V-cutting to the ball, and pivoting on their right foot when they catch the ball. Right-handed and left-handed players should align themselves properly when rising into their shot.

In addition, depending on the skill level of the players or the team, coaches can add a screener to the drill. In this drill the shooter comes off a screen and then dumps the ball down to the screener rather than shooting. This is a great way to teach players the value of setting good screens. More often than not, the players setting the screen will find themselves open after a good shooter has rubbed the defender off them. When setting a screen, always think screen and score.

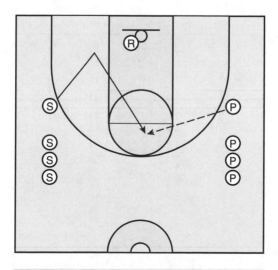

FIGURE 9.8   **Left-to-right V-cut.**

Baseline Shooting

This is another great team drill. As shown in figure 9.9, this drill begins with lines of at least three players positioned under the basket at the free-shot lane. Everyone has a ball except one player, who will be in the front of one of the lines. This player starts out going up the lane line to the elbow. Once at the elbow, the player plants the inside pivot foot and points the toe of the pivot foot in the direction he or she is going. In this case, the player continues on to the other elbow and plants the same inside foot, heel to toe, angling himself or herself to the basket and preparing to step into the shot (shown as S in the diagram).

The player at the baseline standing across from the shooter will deliver the ball so the shooter can catch in rhythm (shown as P in the diagram), and then continues the drill by going outside of the shooter he or she just passed to and planting his or her inside foot at the elbow, preparing to catch and shoot with a consecutive pass delivered from the opposite line. The footwork and movement will be the opposite of the previous shooter because the player will be going the opposite way.

Points of emphasis include making angle cuts, stepping heel to toe, staying low, passing the ball to the shot pocket, calling for the ball, and catching, shooting, and landing on balance. Remember to shoot and stay. This way you can track the long rebound. If you follow your shots, you will often see the ball miss and go right back to where you just shot from. Always shoot and stay. Coaches can have players make a certain number of shots, or they can time this drill to see how long it takes player to make a certain number of shots. Keep the drills competitive. It creates an incentive to improve.

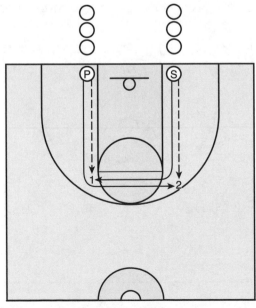

FIGURE 9.9   Baseline shooting.

Sideline Shooting

This drill is similar to the baseline shooting drill, except that it runs from the wing areas in two lines positioned at each free-shot line extended, outside of the three-point line. As shown in figure 9.10, the first shooter begins at the front of one of the lines without a basketball (shown as S in the diagram). He or she V-cuts across toward the opposite line and receives a pass, pivoting heel to toe off the inside foot and rising into the shot. The passer (shown as P in the diagram) then becomes the second shooter, running outside of the player he or she passed to in the opposite direction, and pivoting off the inside foot (the opposite foot).

When the drill is set up in this fashion, you can also add a rebounder. I like adding a rebounder because it stops the shooter from following his or her shot. Remember, you want to teach players to shoot and stay so that they can get long rebounds and key outlet passes or so that they are able to get back on defense. The only time players should follow their shots is when they shoot inside the paint. When you add a rebounder to this drill, they will retrieve the ball and then dribble it, preferably with the weak hand, to the line that the ball was passed from.

FIGURE 9.10 **Sideline shooting.**

You now possess the knowledge necessary to become an effective shooter and scorer when coming off a screen. However, none of this means anything unless you're willing to put in the time and effort to perfect these fundamental skills one by one. How good or great do you want to become?

Not Open? No Problem!

Now that you are in the mindset of catching and shooting on the move when coming off a screen, you must extend what you know about creating off the dribble into the same scenario. Setting good, solid screens is difficult, and aggressive defenders will fight through them and be on your heels as you receive the ball. You should be prepared to put the ball on the floor. Remember that when you dribble, you want to go somewhere with the dribble and you must dribble with your head up. You want to keep your eyes on your target. If your eyes are on your target, you are thinking score. The other benefit of sighting your target is that it allows you to see the width of the entire floor and be ready to find a teammate for a better shot or evade help defenders.

If you are catching on the move from left to right, you will plant the left foot, which is still the inside pivot foot (see figure 9.11a). The only difference is that now you will be immediately dribbling with the outside hand in anticipation of your defender fighting through the screen (see figure 9.11b). In this instance, the outside hand would be your right hand. If you are catching on the move from right to left, you would be doing the opposite, planting your right foot on the catch and immediately dribbling with your left hand, and your inside hand should go into arm-bar position (see figure 9.12 a and b). Now that you have protected the ball, you are prepared to make a move and be the aggressor.

FIGURE 9.11 Shooter catching on the move when going left to right.

FIGURE 9.12 Shooter catching on the move when going right to left.

chapter 10

Shot Charts and Shooting Evaluation

Y ou have the knowledge. You have studied the technique and it is in place, whether you're shooting from midrange or from downtown. You know what it takes to be consistent from the free-shot line. You have an awareness of how to properly execute the bank shot. You know what it takes to fake a defender right out of his or her shoes. You can visualize yourself coming off a screen and hitting that game-winning bucket. You can picture it. You know it. But tell me, can you do it? I'm telling you, you can, but you must chart, and you must evaluate.

Shot Charts

As mentioned in chapter 1, it is important that you keep a shooting journal or shot chart to document your workouts. This is, in many ways, the most crucial step toward evolving into a truly great shooter. Every time I practice, I chart my shots. You can ask me what I shot on any given day of the year, and I can refer back to one of my notebooks and tell you the exact details. Every time you practice, you should do the same. You need to keep track of both your shooting percentage, the number of makes divided by the number of attempts, and the types of shots you put up, e.g., midrange shots, threes on the move, show-and-go right and left. If you do this, you will not only be able to see improvement in your game, but you also will be able to see what you need to work on and improve on. Charting your shots takes discipline. By charting your shots, you will show a desire to get better and the commitment necessary to improve.

In figure 10.1, you will find a sample shot chart you can use to document your workouts and practice routines. In the date and time columns on the left-hand side, record the date and the duration of your workout, e.g., 6/15/2011, 9:30–11 a.m. Use the middle section to jot down notes that pertain to that particular workout. I like to note the gym I was in; maybe it was a YMCA, a high school, or an NBA practice facility. Next note what type of shot you worked on: catch-and-shoot threes, show-and-go right, show-and-go left, free shots, and so on. Finally, if you are working with a partner or a coach, ask if he or she noticed anything about your technique, and then make a note on it. Maybe your coach saw you dropped your balance hand too soon or that most of your misses were short of the rim as opposed to long. You can take this information and make the necessary adjustments in your next workout. Finally, in the shot chart diagram, indicate where you shot from. I usually use dots denoting shooting spots. Below the dots, I write my percentage, e.g., 400/400, 100 percent.

Name:_____

Date	Time	Notes	

			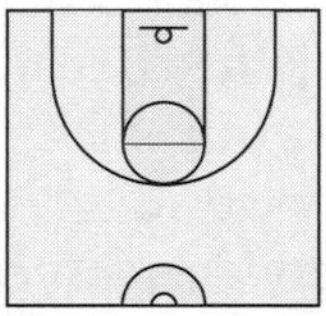

FIGURE 10.1 Sample shot chart.

From D. Hopla, 2012, *Basketball shooting,* (Champaign, IL: Human Kinetics).

Shooting Evaluation

In addition to charting your shots, you must evaluate your shot to have a complete understanding of it. This will be an extension of the evaluation covered at the end of chapter 3 and concerns the gamut of shooting mechanics. Are you gripping the ball properly? Is your shooting arm in an L-shape, allowing you to be a *lifter* as opposed to a *slinger* or *pusher*? How is your knee bend? Is it too little, too much? Are you keeping your head level? You should be able to answer these questions if you are sincere about aspiring to become a great shooter.

The evaluation also concerns your footwork for shooting on the move and shooting off the dribble. Are you pivoting on your inside foot when moving left to right? How about right to left? When you pick up the dribble with your weak hand, are you *loading the gun*? If you have trouble evaluating yourself, have a friend or coach assist you.

Figure 10.2 is a sample shooting evaluation form that you can use to help you evaluate your shots. Once you have evaluated your shot, you can make the necessary adjustments, but note that you should work on this in the off-season rather than in-season. When you make changes to your shot, it will take many practice hours for those changes to pay dividends. Changing technique in the midst of a season is difficult. Between all the games, long bus rides, and your academic schedule, you may find it difficult to discipline yourself to make the needed adjustments to your shooting technique. There is very rarely a quick fix, but if you take the time in the off-season to properly evaluate, work on your skills, and chart the results, you will find that you are more than capable of taking your game to the next level.

FIGURE 10.2　SHOOTING EVALUATION FORM

Name: _____ Date: _____	Yes	No
▶ **Grip**		
Do thumbs form a T?	____	____
Is there a "peek-through," meaning the ball is off palms?	____	____
▶ **Balance Hand**		
Do fingers point toward ceiling?	____	____
Is hand on side of ball?	____	____
Does thumb go back toward ear?	____	____
Is ball off the palm?	____	____

	Yes	No
▶ **Shooting Hand**		
Is ball off the palm?	____	____
Does index finger point to eyebrow?	____	____
Are there wrinkles in wrist, meaning is it fully cocked?	____	____
▶ **Shooting Arm**		
Is arm in an L, rather than an S or V position?	____	____
Is elbow under the ball (i.e. "lifter")?	____	____
Is elbow ahead of the ball (i.e. "slinger")?	____	____
Is elbow behind the ball (i.e. "pusher")?	____	____
▶ **Body Position and Setup**		
Are feet shoulder-width apart?	____	____
Are feet too close together?	____	____
Are feet too wide?	____	____
Are shoulders square?	____	____
Do both heels leave the floor at the same time?	____	____
Do both knees bend the same amount at the same time?	____	____
Does the body go straight up?	____	____
Is the dominant foot forward?	____	____
Is the dominant toe pointing to target?	____	____
Are feet parallel?	____	____
Do feet point toward the basket?	____	____
Does shooter overstride?	____	____
Are head and hips in line?	____	____
Does head stay down and level on the shot?	____	____
Are eyes watching the rim, not the ball?	____	____
Is elbow directly under the ball?	____	____
▶ **Finish**		
Is elbow above the eyebrow?	____	____
Is the shooting hand in the hoop?	____	____

(continued)

Shooting Evaluation Form *(continued)*

	Yes	No
▶ **Finish** *(continued)*		
Is the balance hand up?	____	____
Does balance hand remain still?	____	____
Is there proper arc on the shot?	____	____
▶ **Catching and Shooting: Right**		
Is there an inside-foot plant?	____	____
Does the toe open toward the basket before planting?	____	____
Are the feet squared on the shot?	____	____
Do the feet land in the same spot?	____	____
▶ **Catching and Shooting: Left**		
Is there an inside-foot plant?	____	____
Is there an outside-foot reverse plant?	____	____
Does the toe open toward the basket before planting?	____	____
Are the feet squared on the shot?	____	____
Do the feet land in the same spot?	____	____
▶ **Shooting Off the Dribble: Right**		
Is the player dribbling with the right hand?	____	____
Is there an inside-foot (left) plant?	____	____
Does the toe open toward the basket before planting?	____	____
Does the player pick up the ball with the knees flexed?	____	____
Does the player pick up the ball with two hands?	____	____
Are the feet squared on the shot?	____	____
Do the feet land in the same spot?	____	____
▶ **Shooting Off the Dribble: Left**		
Is the player dribbling with the left hand?	____	____
Is there an inside-foot (right) plant?	____	____
Does the toe open toward the basket before planting?	____	____
Does the player pick up the ball with the knees flexed?	____	____
Does the player pick up the ball with two hands?	____	____
Are the feet squared on the shot?	____	____
Do the feet land in the same spot?	____	____

From D. Hopla, 2012, *Basketball shooting*, (Champaign, IL: Human Kinetics).

Invest in your game and invest in your future. Challenge yourself each and every day. Set short-term and long-term goals to help keep yourself motivated and engaged. Charting your shots shouldn't feel like a burden. This is a part of the process that you should enjoy. All players lose confidence in their game when they become unsure of themselves. Charting your shots provides you with documentation of how you are able to perform a certain skill at a certain point in your playing career. You can then take that information and move forward with a confident understanding of where you excel and where you need to improve.

This all leads to preparation. You have an understanding of how to shoot the ball correctly and how to work out, so now you must have a plan. Before going to the gym, you need to know exactly what you will do and what you will work on. Start every session with form shooting. First, begin with one-hand form shooting. Once finished, add the balance hand. After that, your body and mind should be fully prepared to work on game shots at game speed. Too many players practice slower than game speed and then have trouble making shots during an actual game. Once you have the proper form and technique down, you must shoot shots at game speed.

Finally, remember to do things the correct way. For example, if you want to develop your long-range game, you must not only become adept at shooting the straight-on three, but also shooting the three on the move from left to right and right to left. Catching and shooting on the move requires different footwork. You have to master that footwork, and then practice it at game speed, correctly. If you don't do something right the first time, when are you going to do it right? Perfect practice makes perfect. I've said it before, and I'll say it again: how good or how great do you want to become? The ball is in your court. Now it's up to you to shoot it.

About the Author

Dave Hopla has been the shooting coach for the Washington Wizards and Toronto Raptors. He is considered by many to be the top shooter in the world, regularly knocking down 495 out of 500 shots. He is the world-record holder for the most free throws in one minute with one ball and one passer, having made 26 shots out of 26 attempts. He also holds the record for the most NBA corner three-point shots having shot 18 of 18 with one ball and one passer in one minute. From the NBA three-point line (23 feet, 9 inches), Hopla made 16 out of 17 attempts with one ball and one passer in one minute. These records can be seen on YouTube.

Hopla has held shooting camps all over the world and regularly travels with the NBA for the NBA Basketball Without Borders program. After he joined the Raptors in 2006, Toronto increased its team shooting percentage every month, from 44.2 in November 2006 to 47.5 in January 2007. They also increased their three-point shooting percentage from 30 in November 2006 to 40 in January 2007. In 2007, Dave was hired by the Washington Wizards as an assistant coach for player development. During the 2007 season the Wizards shot a franchise best from the free-throw line (78.8%). While in Washington, the Wizards shot a franchise best from the free-throw line. Dave has worked with many NBA, college, and high school teams and players, including Chris Bosh, Gilbert Arenas, Ben Gordon, Rip Hamilton, Kevin Love, Brandon Jennings, Ray Allen, and Kobe Bryant, as well as several WNBA players, including Diana Taurasi and Sue Bird. Hopla resides in Boothbay Harbor, Maine, with his beautiful wife, Carole, and beautiful daughter, McKenna.

For more from Dave Hopla, please scan this tag (or visit www.tinyurl.com/6mold2d).

You'll find other outstanding basketball resources at

www.HumanKinetics.com/basketball

In the U.S. call 1-800-747-4457

Australia 08 8372 0999 • Canada 1-800-465-7301
Europe +44 (0) 113 255 5665 • New Zealand 0800 222 062

HUMAN KINETICS
The Premier Publisher for Sports & Fitness
P.O. Box 5076 • Champaign, IL 61825-5076 USA

eBook
available at
HumanKinetics.com